Achieving equity in higher education requires clarity of purpose and sustained, purposeful action. The authors of this important new book are steeped in years of experience in both and provide us with insights, information, tactics, and strategies presented so readers may move at their own pace. And move we must to make colleges and universities learning environments for all our students to thrive.

—Sarita E. Brown, President, *Excelencia in Education*

No one at any college or university ought to claim a serious commitment to equity, diversity, and inclusion without first reading this important book and skillfully implementing its authors' smart recommendations. It overflows with conceptual brilliance, credible evidence, and practically useful strategies.

—Shaun R. Harper, Provost Professor and
Executive Director, University of Southern
California Race and Equity Center

From *Equity Talk to Equity Walk* is a master class on moving from the theory of the case for equity to the expansive action that: facilitates equity-mindedness, creates an equitable perspective of the way forward in higher education, and measures equitable outcomes for students. McNair, Bensimon, and Malcom-Piqueux take the reader through the academic scholarship on equity, to the practical application of the same, through their direct, unapologetic approach on the matter, to their first-hand recounting of case studies of their direct work with hundreds of institutions, all in an effort to meet the readers where they are on their equity journey.

From *Equity Talk to Equity Walk* serves as a confirming love letter for the duly-initiated equity walkers as well as a guide and a handbook for the newly initiated equity talkers! This book is required reading for every institutional or policy practitioner whose goal is to facilitate and realize institutional transformation at their college or university, and to achieve equitable outcomes for historically underrepresented, minoritized, and marginalized students seeking to complete a college education within structures and systems that were not created or designed for their success. For all of us seeking to upend those systems and structures, and build a new model for current and future collegians – focused on student success for all students, not the few – this book is for you!

—Yolanda Watson Spiva, PhD, President,
Complete College America

From Equity Talk
to Equity Walk

From Equity Talk to Equity Walk

Expanding Practitioner Knowledge for Racial Justice in Higher Education

Tia Brown McNair
Estela Mara Bensimon
Lindsey Malcom-Piqueux

Association
of American
Colleges and
Universities

CENTER for URBAN
EDUCATION

JOSSEY-BASS™
A Wiley Brand

Library of Congress Cataloging-in-Publication Data is Available:

9781119237914 (Hardback), 9781119237952 (ePDF), 9781119237945 (epub)

Cover Design & Image: Wiley

Printed in the United States of America

FIRST EDITION

SKY10027066_051721

Contents

Acknowledgments

Completing this book would not have been possible without the dedication and commitment of many people throughout this journey. A special thank you to Ben Dedman, associate editor and staff writer, print and digital content, at the Association of American Colleges and Universities (AAC&U), who read drafts of the chapters and provided feedback and editing guidance. Also, thank you to JoEllen Alberts, program coordinator in the Office of Diversity, Equity, and Student Success, who did reference checks and file organization for submission deadlines.

We are additionally grateful to Debbie Hanson, senior project specialist, at the USC Center for Urban Education, for the development and facilitation of data-based activities to assist our campus partners in learning how to make sense of data, and to Deanna Cherry, senior facilitator, for leading the facilitation of activities and dialogue at the Equity Academy held in 2015 in Ft. Lauderdale, Florida.

The work highlighted in this book represents the devotion of countless educators seeking to improve the experiences of students who have been traditionally marginalized in higher education. Thank you for all you have done and continue to do; We want to specifically thank the institutions that participated in AAC&U's *Committing to Equity and Inclusive Excellence: Campus-Based Strategies for Student Success* funded by USA Funds (now Strada Education Network) and Great Lakes Higher Education Guaranty Corporation (now Ascendium Education Group). To Dr. Lorenzo Esters, who served as our program officer and who initially funded this project, thank you for your vision, your confidence, and your willingness to partner with us. The power of our collective action will prevail.

A special thank you to the people in our lives who support us unconditionally. We couldn't do what we do without you.

About the Authors

Tia Brown McNair currently is the vice president of Diversity, Equity, and Student Success and Executive Director for the Truth, Racial Healing, and Transformation (TRHT) Campus Centers at the Association of American Colleges and Universities (AAC&U), where she leads national efforts to improve quality in undergraduate education for underserved students. McNair also directs AAC&U's Summer Institutes on High-Impact Educational Practices and Student Success and TRHT Campus Centers.

Dr. McNair serves as the project director for several AAC&U initiatives: *Strengthening Guided Pathways and Career Success by Ensuring Students Are Learning; Truth, Racial Healing and Transformation Campus Centers*; and *Purposeful Pathways: Faculty Planning and Curricular Coherence.* She also directed AAC&U's national projects on *Committing to Equity and Inclusive Excellence: Campus-Based Strategies for Student Success, Advancing Underserved Student Success through Faculty Intentionality in Problem-Centered Learning, Advancing Roadmaps for Community College Leadership to Improve Student Learning and Success,* and *Developing a Community College*

Roadmap. She is the lead author of the book *Becoming a Student-Ready College: A New Culture of Leadership for Student Success* (with Susan Albertine, Michelle Asha Cooper, Nicole McDonald, and Thomas Major Jr.). McNair is a co-author on the publication *Assessing Underserved Students' Engagement in High-Impact Practices* (with Ashley Finley).

Estela Mara Bensimon is Dean's Professor in Educational Equity at the USC Rossier School of Education and Director of the Center for Urban Education, which she founded in 1999. In 2017, she was elected to the National Academy of Education and she was presented with the 2017 Social Justice in Education Award by the American Educational Research Association. She is also a Fellow of the American Educational Research Association. In January 2018, Governor Jerry Brown appointed Dr. Bensimon to the Education Commission of the States. She also serves on the Campaign for College Opportunity board of directors and is a Distinguished Fellow in the Association for American Colleges and Universities. She earned her doctorate in higher education from Teachers College, Columbia University.

Dr. Bensimon has published extensively about equity, organizational learning, practitioner inquiry, and change. Her most recent books include *Critical Approaches to the Study of Higher Education* (co-edited with Ana Martinez-Aleman and Brian Pusser), which was selected as the 2016 Outstanding Publication by the American Educational Research Association, Division of Postsecondary Education; *Engaging the Race Question: Accountability and Equity in US Higher Education* (with Alicia C. Dowd), *Confronting Equity Issues on Campus: Implementing the Equity Scorecard in Theory and Practice* (co-edited with Lindsey Malcom).

Lindsey Malcom-Piqueux leads the Office of Institutional Research at the California Institute of Technology (Caltech). Her scholarly research focuses on understanding the institutional conditions that advance racial and gender equity in STEM fields. Prior to joining Caltech, she served as the associate director of Research and Policy at the Center for Urban Education at the University of Southern California. She has also held faculty positions at the George Washington University and the University of California, Riverside.

Dr. Malcom-Piqueux's work has appeared in *Educational Researcher*, the *Review of Higher Education, Harvard Educational Review*, among other journals, and in volumes edited by Routledge, SUNY Press, Johns Hopkins University Press, and Stylus Publishing. She earned her PhD in Urban Education with an emphasis in higher education from the University of Southern California, her MS in Planetary Science from Caltech, and her BS in Planetary Science from the Massachusetts Institute of Technology.

Our Institutions

Center for Urban Education

The Center for Urban Education (CUE) leads socially conscious research and develops tools for higher education institutions to produce racial/ethnic equity in student outcomes. Racial and ethnic equity in outcomes remains a problem in higher education despite decades of policies and reforms that seek access, opportunity, and success for African American, Latinx, Native American, and other racially minoritized students. Housed at the USC's Rossier School of Education, CUE works with practitioners and policy makers across the country to devise and implement race-conscious, equity-minded, and context-specific solutions that fundamentally reimagine the kind of change that is needed to achieve equity for racially minoritized students.

Since CUE's founding in 1999, more than a hundred two-year and four-year colleges and universities in 14 states have partnered with CUE to use the Equity Scorecard™ and learn about the concept of "equity-mindedness" that is the foundation for institutional responsibility. More information can be found at https://cue.usc.edu.

Association of American Colleges and Universities

AAC&U is the leading national association dedicated to advancing the vitality and public standing of liberal education by making quality and equity the foundations for excellence in undergraduate education in service to democracy. Its members are committed to extending the advantages of a liberal education to all students, regardless of academic specialization or intended career. Founded in 1915, AAC&U now comprises 1400 member institutions – including accredited public and private colleges, community colleges, research universities, and comprehensive universities of every type and size.

AAC&U functions as a catalyst and facilitator, forging links among presidents, administrators, faculty, and staff engaged in institutional and curricular planning. Through a broad range of activities, AAC&U reinforces the collective commitment to liberal education at the national, local, and global levels. Its high-quality programs, publications, research, meetings, institutes, public outreach efforts, and campus-based projects help individual institutions ensure that the quality of student learning is central to their work as they evolve to meet new economic and social challenges. Information about AAC&U can be found at www.aacu.org.

Foreword

Throughout the course of their innovative book, Tia Brown McNair, Estela Mara Bensimon, and Lindsey Malcom-Piqueux illustrate how white privilege functions at multiple levels in the academy, from high-profile admission scandals such as the Varsity Blues and the proliferation of white supremacist activity on college campuses to dominant norms in constructing class assignments and syllabi that erase the contributions of minoritized groups. Their pivotal scholarship draws urgent attention to the ways in which the prevailing national rhetoric has fostered a new permission structure, encouraging speech and actions that previously would have been condemned as racist, sexist, homophobic, anti-Semitic, ableist or otherwise discriminatory, while simultaneously unveiling underlying practices that contribute to the persistence of racial inequality in the classroom and beyond. In response to these challenges, the authors call for a paradigm shift in language and behavior that places "equity-mindedness" at the center of institutional missions, providing a framework for the development of a comprehensive set of beliefs, values and actions. It is an approach that necessitates both an honest assessment of, and genuine reckoning with, the structural barriers and hidden biases that pervade our own colleges, universities, organizations and associations, mitigating against articulated equity goals as the foundation for student success.

One of the most compelling features of *From Equity Talk to Equity Walk* is that the authors begin by considering the implications of their own language use, participating in the very exercise they are enjoining others to undertake as a means of advancing "engaged inclusivity." Utilizing case studies, examples, and powerful narrative, these researchers remind us that preserving our nation's historic mission of educating for democracy mandates all institutions of higher education to play a leadership role in advancing racial and social justice.

In the process of providing a roadmap for campuses that have the courage to interrogate the reasons why racial inequities remain, McNair, Bensimon, and Malcom-Piqueux highlight the primary importance of arriving at a shared definition of equity. The practical suggestions they pose for how various approaches might be integrated to address complex issues of campus culture and inclusive excellence offer promise for lasting institutional transformation. At the same time, their examination of the political, social and cultural forces that influence higher education practice and pedagogy signals the demonstrated need for colleges and universities to act as anchor institutions, whose success is inextricably linked to the economic, educational, physical and psycho-social well-being of the communities in which they are located and the individuals they seek to serve.

—Lynn Pasquerella

Preface

No one is born hating another person because of the color of his skin, or his background, or his religion. People must learn to hate, and if they can learn to hate, they can be taught to love, for love comes more naturally to the human heart than its opposite.

– Nelson Mandela

We finished writing this book in the same week that men and women in El Paso, Texas and Dayton, Ohio were murdered by two white supremacists fueled by xenophobic hate and bigotry. Much to our dismay these horrific crimes came on the heels of the very public taunting of four congresswomen of color with the epithet of "go back to your countries" and the dehumanization of Baltimore's Black citizens by portraying them and their neighborhoods as infested by vermin. The growing racial tensions in our society and the impact it has had, and will have, on our individual psyche and who we are as a nation, cannot be ignored and dismissed as isolated incidents because they keep adding up. Racism permeates every aspect of our country and the time to address the pervasive impact of ideologies fueled by hate is now. In 1964, our country came the closest it ever has to legislate on behalf of racial justice. The 1964 Civil Rights Act was heralded as a moment in which we confronted in thought and action the wrongs committed in the name of whiteness. We must be willing to advocate for racial justice in all aspects of our society by expanding our knowledge on why and how we keep returning to the place where people are taught to hate instead of love, and where our differences are seen as what divides us, and not what makes us stronger and more knowledgeable.

In this time of public and overt hatred and bigotry it is more important than ever that higher education leaders, faculty, staff, and trustees resolve to speak back and exercise racial equity with vigor and conviction. It is incumbent on higher education to mobilize the power of knowledge and moral leadership to combat the malaise of white supremacy to prepare the next generation of leaders to not repeat the cycle of perpetual harm and trauma we are seeing today.

Chapter 1

From Equity Talk to Equity Walk

A Shared Starting Point

This equity journey begins with you.

Change must happen individually before it can happen collectively. People drive change, lead change, and sustain change. Lasting change happens when educators understand both the meaning of equity and that meaning is represented through personal values, beliefs, and actions. This is why this journey *must* start with you. We want you first to engage in self-reflection on your current equity definition, values, and beliefs before we delve into the explanations and examples of what we mean by equity, and more specifically, racial equity.

How do you define equity? What is your understanding of how equity and equality intersect or are codependent? What are specific examples of how equity is a value for you and to your institution? What motivates you to ensure equity at your institution? How does your understanding of equity translate into your values, beliefs, and actions? Do you have an equity talk *and* an equity walk?

In our experiences working with educators at hundreds of higher education institutions, there is common desire among most to address equity in student outcomes. It is popular to hear, "We want to close the equity gaps in graduation, progression, and retention for our underrepresented students," or "Closing the opportunity gaps in our student outcomes is our equity imperative." For most, this is the place where they enter into the equity conversation. In this context, equity is defined as understanding students' needs and addressing those needs by providing the necessary academic and social support services to help level the playing field so students can achieve their goals. Data are shared and discussed to highlight the equity gaps in student success. The institution makes a commitment to eliminate those gaps, and the interventions to do so are discussed and implemented. In this book, we will emphasize the importance of collecting data on student success outcomes. We realize that it is a critical first step for engaging in conversations about equity. What usually creates angst among some educators is when we turn the discussion to the reason for the equity gaps, and we point out that there are biases and privilege in the language we use to describe students, the way we present data, and the interventions that we propose to eliminate inequities. For our efforts, by focusing first on your willingness to engage in conversations about student success outcomes, we acknowledge that we want to meet you where you are in your current journey, based on the conversations you are having at your institutions. We will hopefully outline a path not only for examining equity in student outcomes, but also for encouraging you to expand your practitioner knowledge for racial equity and justice in higher education. This is what *we* believe *is* the equity imperative.

Educators with an equity talk *and* an equity walk critically examine institutional policies, practices, and structures through a lens that questions why inequities exist to change the educational environment to support the success of students – especially students who have been historically and continuously marginalized in our educational systems. These educators don't just talk about equity, but it is evident in their inquiry-process, decision-making, interactions, and reflections. Equity talk and equity walk educators interrogate the concept of equity and its relationship to equality, including how the paradox of equality requires a critical examination of the historical, social, cultural, and political perspectives that make the concept of equality a misnomer for many in our society, especially minoritized students.

Unfortunately, some educators only have an equity talk, but *not* an equity walk. In this category are the educators who preach equity, but equity values and practices aren't evident in their actions. They have a cursory understanding of equity. In our experiences working with educators across many sectors of higher education, we have seen those who embrace the equity talk, but struggle with the equity walk if the reason behind embracing equity talk stems mostly from it being the current buzzword or hot topic. We don't want to imply that educators who have embraced equity talk do not want to make their respective institutions more equitable. But having an equity talk that will lead to change calls for a comprehensive understanding of what the term means in relation to current and past experiences and institutional contexts. This is where educators in this group are falling short. Often, within this context, when we ask users of the word *equity* what it means for them individually and for institutional practice and change, colleagues on the same campus have various definitions and lack shared understanding of the historical and social contexts that have shaped the need to address equity. This makes it difficult to believe that equity is a pervasive institutional value, especially when campus practitioners have limited knowledge of the multifaceted contexts surrounding the examination of equity.

Other educators have embraced equity talk not from a personal belief but because it is the current buzzword. We love buzzwords in higher education. When we find ones that we believe reflect what we should have as our goals and our values, we quickly add them to our vernacular. The buzz around these words evolves into the reasons we seek to redesign, update, or transform our strategic plans and vision statements to be more like our peer institutions and to join the popular dialogue. Our motivation for engaging in equity talk may contradict our actual beliefs. As pointed out by Estela Mara Bensimon, "It seems like 'equity' is everywhere. ... Equity, once viewed suspiciously as racially divisive and associated with the activism of social justice movements that academic purists disdain as 'advocacy' work, is now being enthusiastically embraced on the academic scene" (2018, p. 95). But, are we truly embracing equity or just a current trend?

There are also educators who struggle with equity talk and have no desire to have an equity walk. This category of educators needs little explanation. These are the people who strongly believe that there are no biases, prejudice, or inequities in our current systems, structures, policies, and practices. They believe that we are in a post-racial society, and equality of opportunity is mainly defined by one's willingness to strive for excellence and work hard. Everyone has an equal chance to succeed, and personal motivation is the determining factor for success.

Educators who fall into this category are not willing to acknowledge that a longstanding belief in a hierarchy of human value has fueled systemic and structural inequities in our country. In addition, they often challenge us by saying we are advocating for students to not be active participants in their education.

For clarity, we believe that success requires reciprocal engagement from students as well as from educators. Students must fully engage in the pursuit of their educational goals, but the institution must also create a learning environment that promotes equity and inclusion by understanding the diversity of the students that it seeks to educate. At the Association of American Colleges and Universities (*AAC&U*), we call this *engaged inclusivity*. Engaged inclusivity "transforms the dialogue on inclusion from general acceptance and tolerance of difference to *active* institutional transformation, based on the belief that the richness of our culture is because of our diversity and a recognition of our common humanity" (AAC&U 2019). And, even for us at AAC&U through our national effort to partner with higher education institutions to establish Truth, Racial Healing and Transformation (TRHT) Campus Centers, we have been prompted by Dr. Gail Christopher, the visionary and architect of the TRHT effort, to reflect on our use of the term *inclusive excellence* as a representation of privilege and hierarchy because it implies that there is a group who (i) has the power to control access to excellence by deciding who is included, (ii) has ownership of what defines excellence, and (iii) requires that others must be invited to be part of this group in order to achieve excellence. Dr. Christopher is encouraging us to use the terminology *expansive* because it breaks down the notion of hierarchy and ownership of excellence to embrace the diversity of ways that excellence can be defined (personal communication, June 25, 2019). Equity work requires high levels of and continuous accountability, assessment, and reflection for all.

This leads us back to the original question: Where are you on your equity journey? It is important that, before you continue reading this book, you engage in reflection on your equity talk and equity walk based on your current understanding of equity. We say your *current* understanding of equity because, in this book, we will explore multidimensional definitions of equity, and we want to meet you where you are. We hope that by figuring out where you are on your equity journey, you will figure out where you want to be by the time you finish reading this book. Do you have an equity talk *and* an equity walk? Do you have mostly equity talk, but *not* an equity walk? Or, are you struggling with *both* equity talk and equity walk?

We wrote this book because we believe in change and that individuals have the power to grow and to evolve. We are motivated to do this work because of the students we encounter on a daily basis that need more educators to have an equity talk *and* an equity walk. We all play a vital role in their pathways to success.

Defining Equity and Inclusive Excellence

The Center for Urban Education (*CUE*) defines equity as "a two-dimensional concept. One axis represents institutional accountability that is demonstrated by the achievement of racial parity in student outcomes, ... [and the] second axis represents a critical understanding of the omnipresence of whiteness at the institutional and practice levels" (Bensimon 2018, p. 97). According to Bensimon et al. (2016), practitioners hoping to be equity-minded "need to consider equity in connection with historical and political understandings of [racial] stratification." Furthermore, "the authentic exercise of equity and equity-mindedness requires explicit attention to structural inequality and institutionalized racism and demands system-changing responses" (Bensimon 2018, p. 97). To examine equity effectively, practitioners must understand how racism and a pervasive belief in the hierarchy of human value have shaped our systems, policies, and practices. To ignore how structures were designed is to ignore the necessary processes for eliminating inequities. We will explain and illustrate this definition of equity and the concept of equity-mindedness in the following chapters through campus vignettes and examples of data analysis.

At AAC&U, equity is a core component of what it means to make excellence inclusive, and it is deeply integrated with diversity and inclusion efforts to improve educational quality and institutional operations:

> The vision and practice of inclusive excellence ... calls for higher education to address diversity, inclusion, and equity as critical to the well-being of democratic culture . ... The action of making excellence inclusive requires that we uncover inequities in student success, identify effective educational practices, and build such practices organically for sustained institutional change.
>
> *(AAC&U n.d.)*

To make excellence inclusive, institutions should have widely shared and commonly understood definitions for diversity, equity, and inclusion that reflect the institutional context and values. For AAC&U, diversity is an understanding of how individual and group differences contribute to the diverse thoughts, knowledge, and experiences that are the foundation of a high-quality liberal education. Inclusion is an active, intentional, and ongoing engagement with diversity across the curriculum, co-curriculum, and our communities to increase awareness, content knowledge, cognitive sophistication, and empathic understanding of the complex ways individuals interact within systems and institutions. Equity prioritizes the creation of opportunities for minoritized students to have equal outcomes and participation in educational programs that can close the achievement gaps in student success and completion.

While these multidimensional definitions for examining equity are varied, they are interdependent and, when utilized collaboratively, they can support comprehensive campus efforts to advance equity and sustainable change. For example, AAC&U's definition of making excellence inclusive focuses on who the students are, equity in student outcomes, and stresses the critical examination of educational environments in which the student will engage. This approach aligns with CUE's efforts to achieve racial parity in student outcomes. Being equity-minded requires examining why inequities exist and understanding how the racialization of institutional practices sustains those inequities. This part of the process – understanding the influence and the historical power of whiteness on structural racism – is often where equity efforts fall short. We believe that the intersection of making excellence inclusive and being equity-minded is the pathway for having a true equity walk. These points will be discussed and illustrated in the following chapters, including using examples from a national project led by AAC&U in partnership with CUE to expand the current research on building institutional capacity to examine equity in student achievement and to identify promising evidence-based interventions for improving student learning and success, and examples from the CUE's work with higher education institutions. We will also illustrate what happens when equity is not viewed as multidimensional, resulting in a limited approach that may not lead to sustainable cultural change at an institution.

Committing to Equity and Inclusive Excellence

Let's start our equity journey by providing an overview of the student success data typically and not typically collected at higher education institutions to initiate conversations about equity. In 2015, as part of AAC&U's Centennial celebration, the association released a number of member surveys to identify opportunities for future work and to assess progress toward shared goals. In AAC&U's report, *Bringing Equity and Quality Learning Together: Institutional Priorities for Tracking and Advancing Underserved Students' Success* (Hart Research Associates 2015), we learned that many institutions are implementing evidence-based practices to advance student success, including requiring student participation in high-impact learning practices (*HIPs*) that support higher rates of persistence and higher levels of achievement of defined learning outcomes (see Figure 1.1).

However, as shown in Figure 1.2, while "many AAC&U member institutions are tracking and disaggregating data on the retention and graduation rates of students from historically underserved groups, far fewer institutions are disaggregating data on

	Required of All Students	Optional
	%	%
First-year experiences that support the transition to college	60	31
First-year academic seminars	52	30
Global or world culture studies	52	41
Diversity studies and experiences	34	53
Service learning in courses	14	79
Learning communities	12	59
Undergraduate research	9	87
Practicums and supervised fieldwork	7	90
Internships	6	91
Study abroad	2	94

Figure 1.1   Data from AAC&U Member Surveys on required or optional high-impact practices at AAC&U Member Institutions.
SOURCE: Hart Research Associates 2015.

Institutions report on their tracking and disaggregation of data on student persistence, graduation, and/or achievement of learning outcomes.

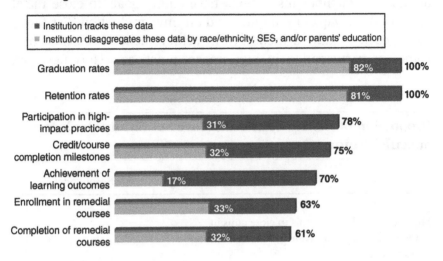

Figure 1.2   Data from AAC&U Member Surveys on tracking and disaggregation of data.

SOURCE: Hart Research Associates 2015.

participation in HIPs or on achievement of learning outcomes" (Hart Research Associates 2015, p. 5). In other words, the institutions are collecting data in the aggregate on student participation in these educational practices – which have been found to be beneficial for underserved student learning and success (Kuh 2008; Kuh and O'Donnell 2013; Finley and McNair 2013) – but they are not disaggregating data to examine questions of equity in student achievement. The same is true for student achievement of learning outcomes. Only 17% of surveyed institutions report that they are disaggregating data on student achievement of learning outcomes. However, when institutions do disaggregate data, they are more likely to look "at differences by race and ethnicity than [students'] socioeconomic status or their parents' level of educational attainment" (Hart Research Associates 2015, p. 5), which provides important data for addressing questions around racial equity.

According to AAC&U's *Bringing Equity and Quality Learning Together* report, and as shown in Figure 1.3, "More than half of AAC&U member institutions have equity goals to close racial and/or ethnic gaps in retention and on-time graduation. Far fewer have goals to address inequities in achievement of learning outcomes or participation in high-impact practices" (Hart Research

Proportion of Institutions That Have Set Equity Goals for Specific Groups

	All Respondents
	%
My institution has set goals to close gaps in **retention and/or on-time graduation** among students. . .	
From different racial and ethnic groups	57
From different socioeconomic groups	36
Whose parents have different levels of educational attainment	27
My institution has set goals to close gaps in **achievement of student learning outcomes** among students. . .	
From different racial and ethnic groups	31
From different socioeconomic groups	24
Whose parents have different levels of educational attainment	14
My institution has set goals to close gaps in **participation in key high-impact learning practices** among students. . .	
From different racial and ethnic groups	23
From different socioeconomic groups	23
Whose parents have different levels of educational attainment	15

Figure 1.3 Data from AAC&U Member Surveys on student persistence, graduation, or achievement of learning outcomes.
SOURCE: Hart Research Associates 2015.

Associates 2015, p. 10). Given AAC&U's mission and focus on making excellence inclusive for all students through access to a high-quality liberal education that prepares them for success in work, life, and productive citizenship, these findings illustrate a need to accelerate efforts to help institutions build capacity to examine questions of equity, specifically for assessing equity in HIPs and student achievement of learning outcomes.

However, if campus educators do not have a widely shared understanding of equity and inclusive excellence, just releasing the member surveys on equity and student success does not automatically translate the vision of committing to equity and inclusive excellence into campus practice. AAC&U and CUE needed to intentionally develop an opportunity for interested campuses to work with both of our organizations to critically explore the definitions of equity and inclusive excellence and the actions needed to eliminate inequities in student outcomes.

In 2015, AAC&U selected 13 institutions (see Figure 1.4) through a competitive selection process to engage in a three-year project sponsored by Strada Education Network (formerly USA Funds) and Ascendium Education Group (formerly Great Lakes Higher Education Corporation & Affiliates) to address the following project goals that emerged as priorities from AAC&U's member surveys:

- Increased access to and participation in HIPs.
- Increased completion, retention, and graduation rates for underserved students (e.g., students who are minoritized based on race/ethnicity, socioeconomic status, adult-learner status, and/or first-generation status).
- Increased achievement of learning outcomes for underserved students using direct assessment measures, including AAC&U's Valid Assessment of Learning in Undergraduate Education (*VALUE*) rubrics or rubrics developed by campuses.
- Increased student awareness and understanding of the value of guided learning pathways that incorporate HIPs for workforce preparation and engaged citizenship.

Anne Arundel Community College (MD)
California State University–Northridge (CA)
California State University–Sacramento (CA)
Carthage College (WI)
Clark Atlanta University (GA)
Dominican University (IL)
Florida International University (FL)
Governors State University (IL)
Lansing Community College (MI)
Morgan State University (MD)
North Carolina A&T State University (NC)
Pomona College (CA)
Wilbur Wright College (IL)

Figure 1.4   Institutions participating in AAC&U's Committing to Equity and Inclusive Excellence: Campus-Based Practices for Student Success Project.

Over the course of three years, the campuses participated in an Equity Academy, webinars, project meetings, conferences, and campus team meetings to build institutional capacity to achieve the project goals. Early in the process, we encouraged the campus leaders to spend significant time discussing who should be part of the campus teams. This is an important step and an element emphasized for teams attending AAC&U's summer institutes for the past 25 years. It is sometimes an overlooked part of the process for providing the necessary structure for examining equity. The teams needed to represent multiple perspectives and key areas of the campus community, including students. The team members needed to be change agents and viewed as campus influencers. They needed to be able to effectively articulate the goals of the effort to their respective campus communities and explain how those goals advanced the institution's strategic priorities and vision.

The Equity Academy was held in collaboration with CUE at the beginning of the project to provide a common starting point for the 13 institutions. It was important for the campuses to come together for a two-day academy not only to begin building a community of practice, but also to have the necessary time to reflect on project goals, to explore individual and shared understandings of equity and inclusive excellence, and to develop first drafts of their campus action plans. Each team had to complete a campus data inventory developed by CUE that included their existing data for the project goal of increasing completion, retention, and graduation rates for underserved students. The Equity Academy used this project goal to illustrate equity-minded data analysis that will be explored in Chapter 3. These data represented common metrics that all campuses had access to prior to the Equity Academy and a shared starting point for engaging in conversations related to equity-minded data analysis.

Prior to attending the Equity Academy, campus teams also received copies of AAC&U's *Committing to Equity and Inclusive Excellence: Campus Guide for Self-Study and Planning* (2015a) and were asked to engage in conversations to assess current practice related to the 10 action steps that were informed by research, member surveys, and campus practice (please note some phrasing has changed from the original document to align with current terminology and institutional values):

1. Know who your students are and will be.
2. Commit to frank, hard dialogues about the climate for minoritized students on your campus, with the goal of affecting a paradigm shift in language and actions.
3. Invest in culturally responsive practices that lead to the success of minoritized students.
4. Set and monitor equity goals and devote aligned resources to achieve them.
5. Develop and actively pursue a clear vision and goals for achieving high-quality learning.
6. Expect and prepare all students to produce culminating or signature work.[1]

---

[1] In signature work, a student uses his or her cumulative learning to pursue a significant project related to a problem she or he defines. In the project, which should be conducted throughout at least one semester, the student takes the lead and produces work that expresses insights and learning gained from the inquiry and demonstrates the skills and knowledge she or he has acquired. Faculty and mentors provide support and guidance. Signature work might be pursued in a capstone course or in research conducted across thematically linked courses, or in another field-based activity or internship. It might include practicums, community service, or other experiential learning. It always should include substantial writing, multiple kinds of reflection on learning, and visible results (AAC&U 2015c).

7. Provide support to help students develop guided plans to achieve essential learning outcomes (see Figure 1.5; AAC&U 2007), prepare for and complete signature work, and connect college with careers.
8. Identify high-impact practices best suited to your students and your institution's quality framework.
9. Ensure that essential learning outcomes are addressed and high-impact practices are incorporated across all programs.
10. Make student achievement – specifically, minoritized student achievement – visible and valued.

For example, the first step, knowing who your students are, involves more than just examining institutional demographic information on the student population. Campus teams in the Committing to Equity and Inclusive Excellence project were asked to examine both quantitative and qualitative data to develop insights into the needs of their current and future student populations: What do your student stories tell you about the work that needs to be done to improve the student experience and educational environment?

We also asked each campus to reflect on their pathways for student success: At what key points on the pathways do students have access to high-impact practices? Is participation optional or required? Can students articulate the value of high-impact practices in relation to career preparation? What makes these practices high-impact, and for whom?

As part of the institute, the campus teams developed action plans based on a template used by hundreds of campuses that have attended AAC&U's Institute on High-Impact Practices and Student Success over the past 10 years (see Figure 1.6). It was important that the campus teams designed action plans with specific equity goals informed by institutional context and data analysis. To promote accountability, the action plans included a space for listing specific team actions with a timeline and, most importantly, how the campus teams planned to measure success. Action plans also asked the campus teams to identify strategies for engaging campus

The Essential Learning Outcomes

★ ★

Beginning in school, and continuing at successively higher levels acroos their college studies, students should prepare for twenty-first-century chanllenges by gaining:

✦ Knowledge of Human Cultures and the Physical and Natural World

- Through study in the sciences and mathematics, social sciences, humanities, histories, languages, and the arts

Focused by engagement with big questions, both contemporary and enduring

✦ Intellectual and Practical Skills, including

- Inquiry and analysis
- Critical and creative thinking
- Written and oral communication
- Quantitative literacy
- Information literacy
- Teamwork and problem solving

Practiced extensively, across the curriculum, in the context of progressively more challenging problems, projects, and standards for performance

✦ Personal and Social Responsibility, including

- Civic knowledge and engagement—local and global
- Intercultural knowledge and competence
- Ethical reasoning and action
- Foundations and skills for lifelong learning

Anchored through active involvement with diverse communities and real-world challenges

✦ Integrative Learning, including

- Synthesis and advanced accomplishment across general and specialized studies

Demonstrated through the application of knowledge, skills, and responsibilities to new settings and complex problems

Note: This listing was developed through a multiyear dialogue with hundreds of colleges and universities about needed goals for student learning; analysis of a long series of recommendations and reports from the business community; and analysis of the accreditation requirements for engineering, business, nursing, and teacher education. The findings are documented in previous publications of the Association of American Colleges and Universities: *College Learning for the New Global Century* (2007) and *The LEAP Vision for Learning* (2011). For more information, see www.aacu.org/leap.

LEAP

Figure 1.5   Essential learning outcomes.
SOURCE: AAC&U 2007.

stakeholders. To effectively engage in equity work, campuses needed to have a transparent communication strategy, an understanding of the barriers to accomplish goals, and strategies for overcoming those obstacles. Equity work cannot be done in isolation or with a select few. It needs to engage the entire campus community.

This template is offered to help you shape your campus action plan. It is not meant to be prescriptive and should be adapted to your specific project goals and institutional context.

Campus Action Plan Goals
Campus actions plans should work toward the following measurable goals to advance equity in student learning and success:

- Increased student access to and participation in high-impact practices (HIPs)
- Increased course completion, retention, and graduation rates for minoritized students (e.g., students of color, socioeconomically diverse students, first-generation students, adult learners)
- Increased achievement of learning outcomes for underserved students using direct assessment measures
- Increased student understanding of guided learning pathways that incorporate HIPs and the value to workforce preparation and engaged citizenship

Institution's Project Description That Addresses the Four Objectives Listed Above
Please explain how the proposed campus project aligns with the institution's strategic vision for student learning and success.

Equity Goals Based on Project Objectives

Targeted Intervention Strategies to Achieve Equity Goals

Barriers to Accomplishment

Opportunities for Support

Engagement Plan for Stakeholders

Communication Strategy

Team Actions and Timeline

Evidence of Success on Each Project Objective
How will you track and monitor progress?

Figure 1.6   Campus action plan template.

For many educators, the Committing to Equity and Inclusive Excellence project and the process described above represent a familiar and comfortable way for engaging in conversations around equity and student success. We intentionally started with a description of this project and decided to use some examples from this effort in this book to meet you where you are. We believe this type of equity work is an important step in moving from equity talk to equity walk, but it is only one step, just like disaggregating data represents one step. Our focus will be on what happens when:

- We start asking about why these inequities exist.
- We start to question privilege and biases in the systems and structures that perpetuate inequities, specifically racial inequities.
- We stop using language that masks who the students really are.
- We stop believing that the accepted norm should be from the dominant culture's viewpoint.

Closing Reflection

In the following chapters, we will examine strategies that emerged from our campus work and from the Committing to Equity and Inclusive Excellence project, including how to take these steps:

- Align strategic priorities with transparent equity values.
- Build a campus culture of equity-mindedness through intentionality.
- Provide faculty and staff development to examine equity.
- Share and use data across all campus sectors.
- Leverage resources to advance equity goals.

We will also raise guiding questions for examining equity from a multidimensional perspective. Not every strategy will be applicable for your institution; institutional context and culture are still driving forces for determining how campuses will engage in equity efforts.

Finally, if you are engaged in conversations about equity in education, you should be keenly aware that disparities in student outcomes persist. This book will not reiterate the plethora of national data on student achievement gaps in higher education. There are numerous publications and reports (e.g. Espinosa et al. 2019; Witham et al. 2015; AAC&U 2015b; Cahalan et al. 2018) that illustrate this common story of student access and success in our educational system. Instead, we will focus on how institutions can examine their data and practices through equity lenses, how they define equity and equity-mindedness, and what that means for campus change. Throughout this book, we have included varying but complementary strategies for examining equity based on the missions of our respective organizations, the work of the institutions that participated in the national project, and our individual campus consultations. All strategies play a role in advancing equity and are interdependent, but examining racial equity is a priority that often gets marginalized. The following chapters will also explore how various approaches must be integrated if we are to truly address issues of equity in higher education. In this process, we will also identify where more work needs to be done as we embrace equity talk to have an equity walk as we seek to build capacity for equity-mindedness among first-generation equity practitioners.

Chapter 2

Building an Equity-Minded Campus Culture

What Is Equity?

Over the past 20 years, the Center for Urban Education at the Rossier School of Education in the University of Southern California has worked with hundreds of colleges and university systems in the implementation of the Equity Scorecard, an organizational-learning and critical-action research process designed for use in colleges and universities (see Center for Urban Education 2019). Its purpose is to produce equity in educational outcomes for racial and ethnic groups that have been subject to oppression and colonization. Evidence teams made up of faculty, student affairs professionals, and administrators conduct action research using data reflecting the status of racial and ethnic equity in access, retention, completion, and participation in opportunities that build students' social capital (e.g., undergraduate research). By observing campus teams as they conducted inquiries of racial inequity (for descriptions of inquiry methods and tools, see Dowd and Bensimon 2015; Bensimon 2007; and the Center for Urban Education website, https://cue.usc.edu), we have identified obstacles that derail institutions' efforts to remedy racial inequity. To counteract these obstacles, the Center for Urban Education coined the term *equity-mindedness* to refer to the mode of thinking exhibited by practitioners who are willing to assess their own racialized assumptions, to acknowledge their lack of knowledge in the history of race and racism, to take responsibility for the success of historically underserved and minoritized student groups, and to critically assess racialization in their own practices as educators and/or administrators.

Not that long ago, the word *equity*, particularly when coupled with race, was viewed by leaders, policy makers, and even philanthropic organizations with apprehension and as potentially divisive. For some, the word conjured images of the activism associated with social justice movements (Bensimon 2018). But now the word *equity* is widely accepted and seems to be as commonplace as *diversity*. One of the motivations for this book is to bring clarity to the meaning of equity and protect it from trivialization and losing its power to shine a light on institutionalized racism.

To bring clarity, we consider simple questions like: What does "equity" mean? Equity for whom? What does it entail in thought and action? What does it mean to perform equity as a routine practice in higher education? And, most importantly, what makes individuals equity-minded? Our intent is to elaborate on these questions from a critical understanding of racial equity premised on the following principles:

- Equity is a means of corrective justice (McPherson 2015) for the educational debt (Ladson-Billings 2006) owed to the descendants of enslaved people and other minoritized populations willfully excluded from higher education.

- Equity is an antiracist project to confront overt and covert racism embedded in institutional structures, policies, and practices (Pollock 2009).
- Equity lets practitioners see whiteness as a norm that operates, unperceived, through structures, policies, and practices that racialize the culture and outcomes of higher education institutions.

These principles are fundamental to the project of racial equity in higher education and demonstrate why it is necessary to adopt a critical race stance toward equity. These three principles allow us to understand why, despite our best intentions to be equitable toward all students, our ways of "doing" higher education continue to produce racial inequality in educational outcomes. And they also illuminate the human and structural obstacles that block the path toward racial equity and the responses that equity-minded practitioners can make to overcome them.

Obstacles Blocking the Path Toward Racial Equity

Equity-minded practitioners do not blame students for their lack of success (a deficit-minded approach), nor do they rely on racial stereotypes or biases to justify or disregard inequitable outcomes. Equity-minded practitioners accept that race and racism are endemic in higher education. In this section, we describe obstacles to making campuses more equitable and provide equity-minded counterexamples.

Obstacle 1   Claiming to Not See Race

The math department chair at Anywhere College notices that a large number of African American and Latinx students who are placed in the department's basic skills math course do not proceed to credit-level math courses. She

(continued)

(continued)

provides the data at a department meeting for discussion. One faculty member says, "This has nothing to do with race." Others say, "I teach students. I don't care whether they are white, black, or purple," or, "Maybe these students are not predisposed to doing well in mathematics."

In the example above, the presentation of disaggregated data by race and ethnicity to raise awareness of racial inequities is met with defensive claims that reject the possibility that race and racism are causes. When individuals claim to not see race, they are actually protecting their professional identity and their feelings of efficacy. They are also protecting themselves from being viewed as racist.

- Saying "this has nothing to do with race" shows a lack of awareness of the ways in which race may play out in the math classroom. For example, the faculty member may not realize that he never interacts with students who are Black or Latinx or that these students rarely participate in class. The faculty member is unable to see or understand the ways in which race plays out in higher education generally and how it plays out in mathematics more specifically.
- Saying "I don't care whether they are white, black, or purple" is a claim of color-blindness as if it were a virtue. The individual who refuses to see that a student is Black, white, Latinx, or Native American is essentially refusing to see the student.
- Saying "these students are not predisposed to doing well in mathematics" is claiming to not see race while

stereotyping minoritized students as not having what it takes to do mathematics.

Equity-Minded Response: Understanding Race Critically

The math department chair at Anywhere College notices that a large number of African American and Latinx students who are placed in the department's basic skills math course do not proceed to credit-level math courses. She rejects the explanation that such students are simply not interested in math. She also recognizes that instructors may not be aware of these patterns of enrollment and may not be trained in culturally inclusive pedagogic practices. To build awareness and to provide training to math faculty, the chair holds monthly brown-bag lunch gatherings to discuss articles and book chapters related to race and math education. Once her faculty are more comfortable talking about race, the math department chair plans on having individual meetings with each instructor, when she will share disaggregated course success rates and discuss self-assessment strategies to help instructors better understand what aspects of their pedagogy might be changed to help ensure equitable outcomes.

Confronting claims of not seeing race requires a critical understanding of race. The math chair in this example sees race critically in several ways:

- By noticing who (by race and ethnicity, Black and Latinx) is failing in the math pathway
- By rejecting the stereotypical explanation that Black and Latinx students are not interested in math
- By considering that faculty may lack the expertise to help Black and Latinx students be successful

Obstacle 2   Not Being Able or Willing to Notice Racialized Consequences

A philosophy instructor at a Hispanic-serving institution generally focuses on canonized Western authors but decides to devote a class day to the work of Chicana scholar Gloria Anzaldúa. The animated response her work generates among the Latina students surprises him. However, he decides to drop her readings from the course because they do not "fit" with the rest of the curriculum. The writing style violates the rules of academic writing. He feels it is more important to teach the canon than try to be inclusive.

- In this scenario, the instructor takes notice of the Latina students' animated response to the work of Gloria Anzaldúa, but it does not move him to self-reflection on his syllabus and teaching practices.
- The instructor falls back on traditional conceptions of how to teach Western philosophy and does not consider alternatives or ways of connecting philosophy to students' knowledge and lives.

Equity-Minded Response: Self-Change in Response to Racialized Consequences

A philosophy instructor at a Hispanic-serving institution generally focuses on canonized Western authors but decides to devote a class day to the work of Chicana scholar Gloria Anzaldúa. The animated response her work generates among the Latina students surprises him. He experiments with incorporating other diverse authors in the curriculum and finds that the class responds positively when exposed to a spectrum of perspectives. The philosophy instructor realizes, in the course of this experimentation, that he almost allowed an inaccurate stereotype about Latinas to justify his use of ineffective classroom practices.

Equity-minded individuals understand that presumptions about cultural predispositions, capacities, abilities, and ambitions are often incomplete or inaccurate. Such practitioners are careful not to employ such presumptions when examining inequities in educational outcomes. They are also aware that their practices, even if they view them as race-neutral, can disadvantage minoritized students (Dowd and Bensimon 2015).

- In this scenario, the instructor takes notice of how Latina students respond to material that speaks to their experience, and he builds on his new awareness to change his syllabus.
- The instructor shows awareness that his initial interpretation of Latina students' silence is based on cultural and racialized stereotypes.

Obstacle 3   Skirting Around Race

Members of the Equity Scorecard team generally avoided naming specific racial groups (e.g., black, Latino, Asian, white), opting instead to use the ambiguous term "diverse faculty." While we certainly recognize that there are multiple forms of diversity, the institutional data on faculty hiring and retention illustrate that a primary challenge centers on recruiting, hiring, and retaining African American, Latina/o, and Native American faculty members. This challenge will be difficult to address if the team does not develop comfort engaging in "racetalk."

(Bensimon, 2015)

(continued)

(continued)

Skirting around race is a reluctance to talk about race in a clear and direct manner, a phenomenon that applies to scholars as well as leaders and practitioners (Harper 2012). In the example above, an excerpt from a memo written to a vice president of a campus implementing the Center for Urban Education's Equity Scorecard, Estela Bensimon called attention to the use of ambiguous language as a substitute for identifying racial and ethnic groups.

Equity-Minded Response: Saying "No" to Racially Coded Language

Leaders at the college referenced above were highly motivated to address racial inequities; nevertheless, they had to unlearn discursive tactics to talk about race without actually talking about it (Pollock 2009).

Equity-minded individuals avoid racially coded (DiAngelo 2011) language such as *at-risk, minority, low-performing, URMs (underrepresented minorities), nonwhite,* or *better-served,* all of which are racialized labels to refer to students who are not North American whites without actually naming them. Equity-minded individuals humanize minoritized students as African American, Latinx, Native American, Hawaiian, Vietnamese, etc. They also understand that lumping all minoritized populations into a single category is another way of avoiding honest race talk.

In a 2016 essay "The Misbegotten URM as a Data Point," Estela Bensimon argued that the use of "underrepresented minorities" dehumanizes the communities it describes:

> *URM is degrading and dehumanizing because it divests racial and ethnic groups of the hard-won right to name themselves and assert their own identity. The movement to be "Black" rather than "Negro" was a political act of*

self-affirmation and agency. It was an act of rebellion and appropriation. "Black" is not simply about color or race; it represents a historical moment of liberation symbolized by Martin Luther King Jr., Malcolm X, the Black Panthers, and intellectual uprisings as symbolized by the writings of Cornel West, bell hooks, Henry Louis Gates, and many more. The emergence of "black" in higher education was an assertion of the right to be present without giving up identity as evidenced in the birth of Black Student Organizations and Black Study programs and departments. Similarly, those grouped within the Hispanic label wanted to acknowledge their nationhood, their indigenous roots, and their connection to usurped lands.

(p. 5)

We recognize that talking about race can be uncomfortable; however, getting in the habit of avoiding euphemisms or racially coded language and using specific terms can signal to others on campus or elsewhere that it is important and necessary to view racial equity as an indicator of institutional effectiveness that must be continuously discussed and monitored. This requires specificity and detail. For example, instead of saying "diverse faculty members or students," name the racial/ethnic groups whose outcomes reflect the attainment of equity and the groups for which the institution needs to perform better. If others use euphemistic terms like *diverse students* or *underrepresented groups,* say to them, "When you mention 'diverse students,' who are you thinking about specifically?" Presidents, vice presidents, deans, and department chairs who probe for clarification can model equity-mindedness and encourage straight race talk.

The colleges that participated in the Committing to Equity and Inclusive Excellence project of the Association of American Colleges and Universities did so voluntarily.

(continued)

(continued)

Their genuine concern and motivation to do better for minoritized students was obvious. One lesson learned from this project is that commitment to bring about change is essential, but it does not guarantee against the use of racially coded language. For example, in their final reports, we noticed that some campuses resorted to racially coded language or ignored race altogether. The inclination toward avoiding direct race talk shows that "not talking about race" is the prevailing norm within higher education, and it will require consistent reinforcement and self-correction to make race-consciousness the preferred norm.

In response to the project's final reports, Bensimon (2018) noted that the word *equity* was included in all of the campuses' reports but often was left undefined and unconnected to racial justice. She made the following recommendations to assist the development of expertise and comfort with race talk among the participants (AAC&U 2018, pp. 53–54).

- To safeguard equity from being trivialized, it needs to be defined very specifically at the level of populations (e.g., black students, Latinx faculty, or black, Latinx, and Native American leaders and trustees) and at the level of outcomes (e.g., admissions, participation in high-impact practices, degree attainment in STEM, transfer from community colleges to highly selective four-year colleges, faculty hiring).
- Adopting a definition of equity that is centered on racial justice does not preclude adopting definitions of other kinds of equity related to gender, income, or sexual orientation; however, these other forms of equity need to be treated separately because inequities based on race

and ethnicity originate from unique historical, socio-cultural, and sociopolitical circumstances, including enslavement, colonization, appropriation of territories, and linguistic hegemony.
- Say no to euphemistic language. To achieve racial equity, it is necessary to clarify and identify who is experiencing equity and inequity. Racially coded language can render racial stratification invisible, and it abets skirting around race.

Obstacle 4   Resisting Calls to Disaggregate Data by Race and Ethnicity

The director of institutional research at a very large, public, multi-campus university system insisted on aggregating Latinx, black, and Native American students into the all-encompassing category of URMs and everyone else into the category of non-URMs. He felt that, at the system level, it was important to have simple metrics and data reporting formats that would not be too cumbersome for busy leaders and board members. He felt that disaggregating data into separate racial/ethnic groups would introduce unnecessary complexity that would dissuade leaders and board members from examining the data. Additionally, the URM category made the system's progress toward closing equity gaps appear more favorable. He reasoned that the individual campuses could disaggregate their data if they wished.

Somewhat related to Obstacle 3, resistance to disaggregating student outcome data by race and ethnicity (e.g., lumping everyone into the URM bucket) is a very common way of hiding racialized patterns in outcomes. It is easier

(continued)

(continued)

for individuals to speak about URMs than black or Latinx students specifically. It is not unusual to hear people say things like, "Our URMs are not doing so well," "URMs have a lower rate of persistence after the first year," or "Our goal is to cut the graduation gap between URMs and Non-URMs by half."

Equity-Minded Response: Resisting the Use of URM by Disaggregating Data

The director of institutional research at a campus that had employed the URM/Non-URM classification for a long time read "The Misbegotten URM as a Data Point" (Bensimon 2016) and realized the importance of making visible the identity of each group to understand their unique and different circumstances. In a memo to the president and vice presidents, she explained that as a generic designation for African Americans, Latinos and Latinas, Asian Americans, Pacific Islanders, and Native Americans, URM represses the critical race questions that numeric data should elicit. To illustrate the importance of keeping each group distinct, she showed that the URM category was misleading since educational outcomes for African Americans were substantially higher than for other groups. Consequently, she said that the continued use of URM was a form of malpractice that obfuscates inequalities between specific racial and ethnic groups (Bensimon). She said, "This institution has always valued evidence that helps us self-correct. The adage 'You don't have to fix what you don't look at' (Carter et al. 2017) has never described who we are."

Obstacle 5   Substituting Race Talk with Poverty Talk

It was the first meeting of a team of 10 instructors and administrators who had been asked by the college president to lead their campus Equity Scorecard initiative. At the meeting, the group was presented with course-level data for English and math courses that showed racial gaps in which students earn a grade of C or higher. One of the team members objected to the focus on race and ethnicity. He said, "It is well established that inequality is a problem of socioeconomic status. Why are we looking at race? I am sure that we would see the same gaps for 'poor whites'."

Insisting that socioeconomic status trumps race is another form of deflecting talk about race. In *What's Race Got to Do with It*, Dowd and Bensimon (2012) shared that one of the questions they were repeatedly asked about their unremitting focus on racial equity is, "What about income?" Or they are told outright that class matters as much as or more than race. At a national conference, the vice chancellor from one of the largest southern university systems emphatically insisted that income – not race – was a more consequential matter.

There is no question that low-income students experience many barriers to higher education. But minoritized students pay a cultural tax (Dowd and Bensimon 2015) that is levied only on American minoritized students who are burdened with the legacies of educational apartheid.

It is less challenging to talk about income than to talk about race, but Lyndon B. Johnson observed that black poverty is different from white poverty (Johnson 1965). One of

(continued)

(continued)

those differences is that low-income African Americans live in concentrated areas of poverty whereas low-income whites are far more spread out (Badger 2015). Racially segregated neighborhoods that are the legacy of redlining practices make it far more likely that a poor black family will live in a neighborhood where many other families are poor, too, creating what sociologists call the "double burden of poverty."

Additionally, studies show that white people are more likely to identify with low-income people because they may know someone who is low-income, or they have experienced poverty. But because whites are more likely to live separately from minoritized groups, they are far less likely to identify with people who are black, Latinx, or Native American.

Equity-Minded Response: Racial Inequality Is a Consequence of Slavery and Conquest

> *Asked by the college president why the Equity Scorecard team was focusing only on racial inequity and not income, the team leader responded, "First, race – unlike income – is visible to the eye. And whether we like it or not, we make judgments – consciously or unconsciously – based on what we see."*

We recognize and accept that race is a socially constructed category. However, as Eduardo Bonilla-Silva points out, race also has "social reality," meaning that "it produces real effects on the actors racialized as 'black' or 'white'" (2006). But we object to the use of such arguments to legitimate color-blindness. Reluctance to speak about race directly is often covered up with the self-righteous assertion that "I don't see race, I just see people," or with the claim (often made in a tone of superiority) that since race is not a biological fact we should not make judgments based on it. We have come across faculty who resist examining the quality of classroom interactions between themselves and students who are not white by claiming that it is not their prerogative to assign identities to students.

Racial inequity – unlike income inequity – was born from slavery and subsequent Jim Crow laws that legalized segregation and mitigated opportunity for African Americans. It was born from genocide and land grabbing that diminished the population and territories of Native Americans, as well as out of the colonization and assimilation projects that sought to "civilize" the "savage natives" (Carter et al. 2017). And it was born from waves of Asian, Latinx, and Pacific Islander migration, some of which was sanctioned by the American government (e.g., through the Immigration Act of 1965 and asylum seeking) and some of which was not. For all people of color, racial inequity was born from policies and practices that were not designed for their benefit but for the dominant population of whites. Racial inequity was also born from policies and practices that actively sought to exclude, marginalize, and oppress people of color. As President Lyndon B. Johnson said during his 1965 commencement address at Howard University:

> But freedom is not enough. You do not wipe away the scars of centuries by saying: Now you are free to go where you want, and do as you desire, and choose the leaders you please.
>
> You do not take a person who, for years, has been hobbled by chains and liberate him, bring him up to the starting line of a race and then say, "You are free to compete with all the others," and still justly believe that you have been completely fair.

(continued)

(continued)

Thus, it is not enough just to open the gates of opportunity. All our citizens must have the ability to walk through those gates.

This is the next and the more profound stage of the battle for civil rights. We seek not just freedom but opportunity. We seek not just legal equity but human ability, not just equality as a right and a theory but equality as a fact and equality as a result.

Addressing racial inequity is therefore an act of justice that demands system-changing responses and explicit attention to structural inequality and institutionalized racism.

Obstacle 6   The Pervasiveness of White Privilege and Institutionalized Racism

A black woman administrator was an active participant at an institute on inclusive pedagogies in science and mathematics that included about 50 faculty members from departments across campus, all but 3 of whom were white. In sessions, the woman provided examples of ways in which black and Latinx students were subject to microaggressions in and out of the classroom. She also provided many useful and practical examples that helped the institute directors situate their content in actual situations. Before breaking for lunch, the institute directors received a message from one of the institution's vice presidents advising them that other participants had complained that the black woman was monopolizing the conversation and that the others did not feel "safe" to participate. The black woman was admonished by her supervisor for dominating the conversation. The incident silenced the three black women for the rest of the institute.

The scenario above, which is based on an actual situation experienced by CUE facilitators, depicts strategies borne out of white privilege in the following ways:

- The complaining faculty and the administrators they complained to were white.
- The white faculty, rather than saying they did not want to listen to the black woman's analysis of the racial consequences of their practices, exercised their "white privilege" to make a kind of complaint (e.g., lack of objectivity, emotional, one-sided) that is often used to silence minoritized groups.
- The complaining faculty felt the right to make their discomfort known and likely did not anticipate being ignored. No one said to them, "Don't take it so personally" or "You are being too sensitive" – responses that may have been given if the complainants were black.
- The black woman had insider knowledge about the classroom experiences of minoritized students. Her knowledge enriched the content of the institute and provided teachable opportunities for STEM faculty to learn equity-mindedness. However, her knowledge was dismissed as not objective. The black woman was an administrator, but in the eyes of STEM faculty she was not viewed as an authority.

Equity-Minded Response: Remediating Whiteness in Practices

The administrator in the scenario above, who in fact wants to create an affirming culture for racial equity, could have considered the following actions:

- The administrator could have gone to the meeting and observed the racial dynamics on her own, including

(continued)

(continued)

actually counting by race and ethnicity who spoke and what they spoke about.

- The administrator could have viewed the episode as a "teaching moment" and scheduled a conversation with the complainers about white privilege, racialization, and the validity of the lived experience of people of color as a source of expertise.

- The administrator could elevate the expertise of minoritized staff members by deferring to them, asking for their opinion, and positioning them in roles of authority.

Most faculty and administrators in higher education are white, and when minoritized populations speak out on issues of race and racism they are often described as "discontent," "trouble makers," "disruptive," or "making everything about race." Hardly anyone in higher education would take issue with the desirability of increasing faculty and leadership diversity – but only as long as "diverse newcomers" do not disrupt established institutional norms, practices, and policies. In the scenario above, the black administrator was perceived by her white colleagues as violating the norms of "civil discourse" – bringing up issues that caused them discomfort or that challenged their versions of reality. She also violated academic norms that privilege faculty expertise over the expertise of staff. Most white administrators lack the knowledge, experience, or awareness to consider the incident above as a reflection of veiled racism and white privilege.

Obstacle 7   Evasive Reactions to Racist Incidents

Campus racist incidents have become far too frequent. On a regular basis, Inside Higher Ed and the Chronicle of Higher Education report stories about students engaging in "blackface" (Mangan 2019), clamoring to build the "wall" (Bauer-Wolf 2019), singing racist songs (Berrett 2015), and making all manner of racially insensitive and offensive remarks. Campus leaders often respond to such incidents by parroting the standard phrase, "These are not our values." Below is a different kind of response to such incidents.

Equity-Minded Response: Calling Attention to the Saliency of Whiteness

In a special meeting of the faculty and students that was prompted by a series of racist incidents, the president (a scholar of critical race studies) gave a candid speech on "whiteness" as the root cause of such incidents. He told the audience, "Despite racial integration and increased access to higher education for minoritized populations, whiteness and institutionalized racism are omnipresent in the curriculum, hiring practices, definitions of merit and quality, enrollment patterns by discipline, representation in prestige- and opportunity-enhancing programs and activities (e.g., undergraduate research, honors programs), leadership, and boards of governance. Whiteness is not only present in predominantly white institutions; it is just as evident in minority-serving institutions like ours, because we, even with our very best intentions, have been socialized into an

(continued)

(continued)

academic culture that was borne out of the experience of white males. Even though higher education is no longer for whites and males only, their imprint lives on in our traditions as well as our definitions of collegiality, merit, and fit."

Instead of saying that the racist incidents do not "represent our values," this president spoke candidly about "whiteness" as the condition that enables public and unabashed expression of racism. Most higher education leaders are white, and noticing the pervasiveness of whiteness is not normally expected of them. Understanding whiteness as privilege and power is not something they have been taught, and it is not a competency they are expected to demonstrate. In an interview for a higher education position, they are not likely to be asked how they guard against being blinded by white privilege.

To address racial inequity in higher education, whiteness has to be called out directly. Doing so requires a willingness to disrupt the "culture of niceness" (McIntyre 1997) and collegiality that faculty and others are expected to observe. It also requires that white colleagues do not resort to the tactics of white fragility (DiAngelo 2011) to avoid the discomfort of race talk.

In a predominantly white higher education system, the dismantlement of whiteness and institutionalized racism requires white people to feel anger, distress, and outrage with a system that unfairly advantages them (McIntosh 2019). Men, McIntosh observes, may be sympathetic to gender inequality; however, they rarely feel distressed about the unearned advantage and dominance they gain from it (McIntosh 2019). In higher education, the power to bring about change is mostly in the hands of white leaders, trustees, and faculty. They may embrace the ideals of diversity, inclusiveness, and equity and commit to new initiatives to help "disadvantaged minorities." However, their good intentions and benevolence have not led to the dismantling of the structures and policies from which they benefit.

Below are examples, inspired by the work of Peggy McIntosh (2019), of the ways whiteness shapes the experience of white college students differently than for minoritized students.

- White students, leaders, and practitioners, for the most part, do not see whiteness as a racial identity.
- White students can take advantage of faculty office hours without feeling their intelligence or potential will be compromised.
- Most white students don't have to ensure that they are using "proper English" when speaking out in class to avoid being stereotyped.
- White students do not view group work with apprehension because they don't expect to be left out.
- White students can find off-campus housing without feeling scrutinized.
- White students often attribute their academic achievement to effort and hard work and rarely notice or acknowledge the assistance they have received from teachers and social networks.
- White students feel they are entitled to receive extra academic support and not feel stigmatized.
- White students can usually be sure they and their experiences will be reflected in the curriculum.

Obstacle 8   The Incapacity to See Institutional Racism in Familiar Routines

During a project supported by the Ford Foundation and the Bill and Melinda Gates Foundation, the Center for Urban Education worked to implement the Equity Score-card in Colorado colleges. Through the methods of partici-patory critical action research, the math department at the Community College of Aurora was engaged in a variety of inquiry activities to help them see that their practices were racialized. One of the inquiry activities focused on the hir-ing of math faculty. In answering the question, "How do you hire faculty?" and by breaking the routine practice of hiring into its most minute details, the chair of the math depart-ment, James Gray, realized that in the 10 years he served as chair he had not hired a single African American. Reasons for this included the structure of hiring (with explicit and implicit rules), the external community he relied on to iden-tify candidates (which consisted of an all-white network of math department chairs), and the artifacts that were integral to the hiring process (such as interview guides). Through processes that he took for granted and had never examined through the lens of racial equity, James was effec-tively ensuring that there were no African American candi-dates in the candidate pool

(Felix et al. 2015).

Racism is often thought to be an act that is committed by individuals; however, the most pernicious form of racism is routinely created and reinforced through everyday practices (Essed 1991) such as hiring, program review, what gets included in strategic plans, what data gets reported, tenure and promotion reviews, syllabi and curriculum, the agendas of boards of trustees, and even in the content of websites and other forms of communication used by institutions.

Equity-Minded Response: Self-Remediation of Routine Practices

By holding a mirror to the hiring practices and examining them from the standpoint of racial equity, Gray came to the conclusion that the hiring system he maintained for ten years was perfectly designed to not hire faculty of color (Felix et al. 2015). The process of studying hiring as a racialized structure enabled Gray to make major changes that resulted in the hiring of black and Latino faculty. One of the changes was to ask all candidates to demonstrate how they would explain the syllabus on the first day of class. This simple exercise made it possible to differentiate among candidates that explained the syllabus as a contractual document and those that would use the syllabus to connect with students and reduce their fears about math.

(Felix et al. 2015)

Gray was able to remediate hiring practices because he admitted that they were designed to advantage white candidates. As the math department chair, he was willing to bring about changes that many others in higher education are afraid to try because they fear violating the norms of collegiality and civility. Rather than saying he had not hired African American faculty because they did not apply or because the pool was limited, he admitted to relying on an all-white network for potential candidates. Gray became an equity-minded leader because he did not reject the concept of whiteness and did not attempt to justify his decisions.

McIntosh's (1988, 2019) analysis of whiteness offers important lessons for all higher education leaders and practitioners, particularly for whites who aspire to equity-mindedness. We have been taught to understand racism as "something that puts others at a disadvantage" but, as discussed above, we are not taught to see how the privileges accrued by whiteness produce advantages. At times, equity

(continued)

(continued)

talk in higher education is centered on remediating racial inequities in educational outcomes. We want to close equity gaps in math for black males. We want more women of color to succeed in STEM fields. We want more Native American and Hawaiian students to transfer to four-year colleges and earn bachelor's degrees. These are worthy and necessary goals. However, framing equity exclusively as a project to remediate the disadvantages experienced by minoritized populations (e.g., closing gaps) falls short of equity-mindedness. The higher education disadvantages accrued by minoritized populations cannot be remedied without leaders and practitioners seeing whiteness as a problem that has to be addressed. Inequity in educational outcomes for minoritized students is a disadvantage they accrue as a consequence of a system based on conceptions of academic achievement that advantage white students and impose a cultural tax on minoritized students (Dowd and Bensimon 2015).

Obstacle 9   The Myth of Universalism

The president of a Hispanic-serving institution community college with a student body that is 60 percent Latinx was excited to announce that the college received a $2 million grant to implement adaptive learning technology. "This grant will enable us to help all of our students by providing them with the tools and resources to complete their course work in a timely manner," the president said. "I am confident that with this grant we will be able to ensure success for all students, erase equity gaps, and increase transfer rates to four-year colleges." When he asked if there were any questions, the chair of the Chicano and Chicana Studies department stood up. "Congratulations on getting this *grant for our college," he said. "I am sure it will help many students. But I have a concern. It sounds as if 'adaptive learning technology' is being presented as a solution that is good for 'all' students. We seem to be ignoring that our students are not all the same. It strikes me that 'adaptive learning technology' is a solution focused on the reality of white students who have easy access to the internet. In the past, we have tried many other 'solutions' to address student success and most have had limited impact. The common element among these solutions is that they have been designed by well-meaning innovators who don't realize that their way of understanding student success is not the universal understanding."*

Universalism is a prominent characteristic of whiteness (DiAngelo 2011) based on the assumption that a white person's view of the way things are is objective and representative of reality (McIntosh 1988). Universalism is also a prominent characteristic of the ways that higher education achievement is theorized, measured, and portrayed. The most obvious example of universalism in higher education is in the propensity to speak of "all students" as if their status as students makes them all the same. Examples of universalist reasoning include a faculty member asserting, "I care about all students"; a president repeating the adage, "A rising tide raises all boats"; or a policy maker saying, "We are all humans" in defense of a race-neutral position. For example, trending higher education initiatives such as pathways, predictive analytics, intrusive advising, dual enrollment, and promise programs assume that they will benefit all students. They fail to see that they might be harmful and worsen disparities. According to Robin DiAngelo, "Universalism functions to deny the significance of race and the advantages of being white. Further, universalism

(continued)

(continued)

assumes that whites and people of color have the same realities, the same experiences in the same contexts (i.e. I feel comfortable in this majority white classroom, so you must too), the same responses from others, and assumes that the same doors are open to all" (2011, p. 59).

Equity-Minded Response: Being Critically Race Conscious

Azul State College is considered a national leader for incorporating racial equity as a key element of its dual-enrollment program. However, Azul's dual-enrollment program was not always critically race conscious. Like most dual-enrollment programs, Azul's administrators assumed that if they put it in place then local high schools would take advantage of it. At the end of the first two years of implementation, the chair of African American Studies asked for data on who participates in dual enrollment. The data was a shock. None of the neighboring high schools with predominantly black and Latinx student bodies participated. The majority of the participating students were at a suburban high school in a working-class neighborhood that was predominantly ethnic white (e.g., Italian American and Irish American) and had a growing East Asian population. The data was a catalyst for infusing racial equity into the dual-enrollment program. The key practices to accomplish this included setting dual-enrollment goals by race and ethnicity based on the minoritized population at each high school, identifying and hiring high school teachers of color to teach the dual-enrollment courses, a comprehensive review of the syllabi used in dual-enrollment courses to assess them as exemplars of cultural relevance and inclusivity, a required training on equity-minded teaching for all dual-enrollment instructors, and an annual report detailing the state of equity in the dual-enrollment program.

Being critically race conscious means reminding oneself and others that when the reference point is all students, it is much more likely to conjure the image of white students than students from minoritized groups. Being critically race conscious means interrogating phenomena from the standpoint of race:

- In what ways could this practice, program, or policy disadvantage minoritized students?
- Who, by race and ethnicity, is most likely to benefit from this practice, program, or policy? Why?
- How did the architects of this practice, program, or policy take racial equity into account?
- Who, by race and ethnicity, might not meet criteria that determine who qualifies (to be hired, to be accepted into an honors program, or to receive promise program benefits)?

Obstacle 10   Seeing Racial Inequities as a Reflection of Academic Deficiency

When asked by a researcher at the Center for Urban Education why more Latinx students were not being successful in STEM fields, a STEM professor responded by describing Latinx students: The students don't have much education background and they don't know what college is like; they think college is an extension of high school, so they don't realize how much work they need to put in.

The Center for Urban Education researchers have observed that practitioners, like the professor above, are far more likely to hold minoritized students responsible for

(continued)

(continued)

worse outcomes than their own practices and biases. When instructors see data that show minoritized students, particularly black, Latinx, and Native American students, performing poorly in the courses they teach, they will say things like, "They were not expecting the course to be rigorous," "They were unprepared for college-level work," "They don't know how to study," "They are not motivated," "They don't value education," and so on. The Center for Urban Education labels these attributions as deficit-mindedness, meaning that instructors view students as lacking the essential skills and attributes they associate with academic success, motivation, self-efficacy, individual effort, and academic integration (Bensimon 2007).

Deficit-mindedness can be detected in comments that practitioners and others make about the perceived shortcomings of African American, Latinx, Pacific Islander, and Native American students, such as having attended poorly resourced schools, growing up in low-income communities, being raised by single-parent households, coming from families that do not value education, and the like. That is, these shortcomings are a "natural" outcome of these students' backgrounds, and addressing attendant inequities requires compensatory programs that "fix" students and teach them how to assimilate into the dominant college culture. Focusing on student characteristics can make it seem as if higher education's policies and practices have played no role in producing racial inequities.

There are many code words for deficit-mindedness:

- Students are underprepared.
- Their culture does not value education.
- Their parents expect them to work.

- They don't know how to be students.
- They don't know how to study for a test.
- They read the book, but they don't understand it.
- They lack self-regulation skills.
- They got by in high school and don't realize college is different.
- They have no idea what it is to be a college student.
- They may say they aspire to transfer but have no understanding of what it entails.
- Their language arts skills are lacking.
- They do not know how to read or take notes.

A deficit-minded perspective of student success can also be evident in the language of syllabi, particularly in open access institutions that attract large numbers of first-generation minoritized students. Syllabi may adopt a tone that anticipates students to be low performers. Instructors who have acquired a deficit mindset also tend to write rules and expectations that come across as cold, uncaring, and even dehumanizing. For example, some syllabus statements – "If you cannot dedicate at least two hours of study for each hour of class then you should drop the course" – do not create a positive or welcoming learning context. Even if it was intended to be helpful, it sounds reproachful, uncaring, and indifferent. Deficit-minded instructors often write their syllabi in ways that tell students the many ways in which they can fail the course rather than succeed.

Equity-Minded Response: Examining Why Practices Work So Much Better for White Students than for Minoritized Students

A first-generation Latino STEM professor at a flagship public university noticed that his colleagues were not likely to select Latinx students to work in their labs. He said,

(continued)

"They get impatient because the students went to high schools without science facilities, so they have not learned the basics. Getting into a lab is really essential to pursue a career in STEM. It is the best way for students to develop a science identity. So . . . on my own time, I started a lab boot camp in the summers to get the students ready to work with my colleagues. It has worked well so far. We are a Hispanic-serving institution, and I just wish my colleagues would be willing to invest more time in our Latinx students. I see myself in the students, and in them I see the future faculty."

(Adapted from Bensimon et al. 2019)

Equity-mindedness upends the analysis of racialized patterns of inequality. From an equity-minded perspective, questions such as these are rejected because their framing situates lower performance on Black, Latinx, and Native American students: Why are the grade-point averages (GPAs) of black students the lowest? Why do so many Latinx students fail college-level math? Why are Native American students' relationships with faculty so weak?[1] The framing of these questions encourages "solutions" that aim to fix minoritized students by providing them with add-on, compensatory services such as intrusive counseling and remediation.

Equity-minded practitioners shift the attention away from the student onto themselves and their practices, reframing racialized gaps in performance as an institutional dysfunction stemming from underpreparedness to perform as effectively for black, Latinx, and Native American students as for whites. From an equity-minded perspective, racialized gaps are a catalyst to ask questions such as: What courses contribute to the lower GPAs of black students? What causes

---

[1]These questions were inspired by deficit-oriented questions in Shaun Harper's "An Anti-Deficit Achievement Framework for Research on Students of Color in STEM" (2010, 68).

these courses to underperform for black students? How many sections of college-level math are offered? Which among these sections perform well or underperform for Latinx students? Why do they have differences in performance? Why are faculty members more likely to establish relationships with white students? What can they do to establish relationships with Native American students? In what ways do faculty discourage Native American students from seeking them out?

Establishing a culture of equity-mindedness depends greatly on leaders who go beyond rhetorical praise for diversity, inclusiveness, and equity. It requires leaders who model the tenets of equity-mindedness in language and action. Below are some examples.

Modeling equity-minded data interpretation	
A community college president looking at the latest report on transfer patterns to four-year institutions . . .	
DOES NOT SAY: International students have over-the-top transfer rates. Latinx students just don't transfer.	DOES SAY: What is it about the way we "do transfer" that makes it work so much better for international students than for Latinx students?
DOES NOT SAY: International students come here motivated to excel and transfer to the best institutions.	DOES SAY: Is it possible that faculty are biased toward international students because they are from high-income backgrounds? Is it possible that faculty may feel they have more in common with international students than with first-generation, low-income Latinx students?

(continued)

(continued)

DOES NOT SAY: We need to recruit more international students because they really make our transfer rates look great and it will help us move up the rankings of good transfer colleges.	DOES SAY: We need to hire faculty and staff who identify with Latinx students, including faculty from this community who may have been successful transfer students themselves. We need to learn if and how faculty and staff develop transfer aspirations in Latinx students. We need to learn how we develop transfer knowledge among Latinx students.
DOES NOT SAY: Latinx students are not interested in transfer. They want well-paying jobs as soon as possible. They are expected to help their families.	DOES SAY: We need to treat every Latinx student as a transfer student. Every department will be asked to create a plan for enhancing Latinx transfer. We will initiate a comprehensive year-long seminar to teach everyone the competencies needed to be an equity-minded institutional agent for transfer.

What Should Institutions Do Next?

Experience has taught us that equity-mindedness does not come naturally. It requires a knowledge base. It takes a lot of intentional practice. It is impossible to craft an agenda for racial equity in higher education without acknowledging that, with the exception of Historically Black Colleges and Universities, most colleges and universities in the United States since the founding of Harvard University in 1636 were created for whites. Many of the universities that represent the greatness of US higher education were built by slave labor, among them the University of Virginia, Georgetown University, Yale, Harvard, and many more (Wilder 2013).

We recognize that even when terms such as *institutionalized racism, whiteness, race-neutral, color-blind,* and *equity-mindedness* are understood in theory, it is far more challenging to identify them in our own actions or the actions of others, in our routines or the routines of our colleagues, departments, and institutions.

We could say that learning equity-mindedness is like learning a new language, but that would be too simplistic. Learning a new language entails repetition, memorizing rules, mimicking intonation, and pronunciation. Learning equity-mindedness is much more complex. It requires that we (particularly those of us who possess the privileges of whiteness) realize that our actions – despite our best intentions, despite not being overtly racist, and despite our commitment to treating everyone equally – may still be harmful to minoritized students.

Being equity-minded does not come naturally. One strategy to move toward equity-mindedness is to evaluate one's work against the following questions:

- In what ways could this practice, program, or policy disadvantage minoritized students?
- Who, by race and ethnicity, is most likely to benefit from this practice, program, or policy? Why?

Chapter 3

Using and Communicating Data as a Tool to Advance Equity

Equity-Minded Data

Higher education institutions use data in increasingly complex ways. Virtually all US institutions have long reported basic information about their students, programs, and personnel to remain in compliance with federal, state, and/or system requirements. A growing proportion of campuses also use data to inform institutional action and decision making. Once confined to offices of institutional research, a range of analytical tools and techniques including performance indicators, data dashboards, and predictive analytics are now deployed campus-wide in an effort to improve effectiveness and advance institutional priorities. As data have become more readily available and accessible, faculty, staff, and administrators are turning to data as a means to inform their practice. This evolving and expanded use of data enables institutions to assess how well they are fulfilling their missions and to identify areas that require institutional improvement. One such area is eliminating race-based inequities in retention and completion.

As detailed in previous chapters, achieving educational equity remains a significant challenge for many two- and four-year colleges and universities. These institutions often seek to employ data-based approaches to tackle equity-related challenges. Indeed, it is crucial that institutions gather and analyze qualitative and quantitative data in order to understand student experiences, learning, and outcomes. Equally important, however, is the process during which practitioners reflect on and make sense of data to inform their actions. Simply consulting or examining data is insufficient. The perspective that practitioners use to interpret equity gaps, the questions that their interpretations lead them to ask, and what follows those questions matter as well. For example, a faculty member who views equity gaps as originating from student deficits will take a different course of action (or inaction) than colleagues who ask themselves how their own practices create or exacerbate the inequities in outcomes apparent in the data. Failing to use data in equity-minded ways can stymie institutional learning and change, leaving equity gaps unchanged.

This chapter discusses how data, when used in equity-minded ways, can help practitioners to understand and address inequities experienced by racially minoritized populations. From institutional-level indicators to practitioner-designed measures of what is occurring in the classroom, data can be an indispensable tool to uncover where equity gaps exist and inform the specific steps that can be taken to close them. The strategies outlined in this chapter originate from the work of the Center for Urban Education (*CUE*). With over two decades of experience working directly with practitioners, institutions, and systems to eliminate racial inequities in outcomes by remediating educational practice, CUE researchers have developed effective approaches and tools to use data to make equity gaps visible and encourage equity-minded sensemaking and action by practitioners. These approaches have been shown to spur practitioner learning and advance racial equity. This chapter also provides specific examples that illustrate common barriers that institutions face when trying to use data as a tool to advance equity.

How Disaggregating Data Makes Inequities Visible

Being equity-minded involves examining data disaggregated by race, noticing racial inequities in outcomes, and making sense of that data in critical ways (Bensimon 2007; Bensimon and Malcom 2012; Dowd and Bensimon 2015; Malcom-Piqueux and Bensimon 2017). Disaggregating institutional data is a critical first step to addressing inequities, because doing so allows practitioners to "see" differences in student outcomes (Bauman 2005). As described in preceding chapters, the concept of equity is theoretically rich, nuanced, and rooted in the ideal of racial justice. When examining quantitative data, equity is operationalized as "parity in representation and outcomes for racially minoritized groups" (Bensimon 2007; Bensimon and Malcom 2012). The goal of the "equity as parity" standard is that all racial/ethnic groups achieve an outcome rate equal to that of the highest-performing group. Thus, an institution can be said to have achieved equity when institutional data show no disparities in educational outcomes (e.g., degree completion rate, retention rate, course success rate) and reflect the proportional participation of racially minoritized students in all levels of an institution (e.g., high-status special programs, high-demand majors, honors programs).

Groups of students whose outcomes fall below that of the highest-performing group are said to be experiencing equity gaps. Setting the highest-performing group as the benchmark establishes an expectation that institutions should serve all racial/ethnic groups at the same level as the group who, as shown by data, is best served by the structures, processes, and peoples represented by each metric.

Determining whether inequities exist requires that data be disaggregated by race/ethnicity. Simply reporting averages obscures any differences in outcomes that might exist, rendering them invisible. Figure 3.1 illustrates the importance of disaggregation, using a simplified example. The data in the figure reflect a fictitious institution's degree completion rate. On the left side of the figure, the completion rate (60%) is reported in the aggregate. On the right, the completion rates for Asian, Latinx, Black, and white students

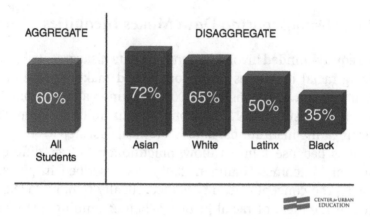

Figure 3.1 Disaggregating data reveals equity gaps.
SOURCE: Center for Urban Education.

are reported separately. Using the standard of equity as parity, it is clear from the disaggregated completion rate data that Black and Latinx students are experiencing a sizable equity gap. These gaps only become visible when the data are disaggregated.

Though there is some value in examining outcome data in the aggregate, it is limited in an institution's pursuit of racial equity. Returning to the example above, examining the overall completion rate may prompt practitioners to note that the outcome falls below their expectations or what they hope to achieve as an institution. The aggregate measure may initiate institutional efforts to raise graduation rates, but it provides little guidance on where to begin. By not disaggregating data, practitioners at that institution would not see that efforts to improve outcomes should first focus on closing the equity gaps experienced by Black and Latinx students. Doing so would have the effect of raising the average *and* better serving students who have been historically marginalized from higher education.

Data can be disaggregated in any number of ways. Institutions have long reported outcome data disaggregated by gender, and in recent years, disaggregating by socioeconomic status and first-generation status has become more common. Disaggregation in and of itself is not a novel practice. However, purposefully disaggregating top-level and fine-grained outcome measures by race as an organizational routine is not as common as it needs to be to make progress on the equity challenges faced by the nation's higher education system.

Disaggregating data by race may cause pushback among some higher education practitioners. Over the course of CUE's work with institutions and practitioners across the country, Bensimon and her colleagues have described encounters with resistance from some practitioners who argue that disaggregating data in this manner "makes everything about race." Other practitioners may oppose disaggregating data by race for other reasons, believing that doing so will reinforce stereotypical conceptions of racially minoritized groups who experience equity gaps. No matter the direction from which opposition to disaggregating data by race originates, those who argue against doing so may be attempting to alleviate their own personal discomfort or to avoid making waves and causing discomfort in others.

Indeed, making the equity gaps visible can be disquieting – this is, in large part, the point. Seeing race-based equity gaps is intended to "create an 'indeterminate situation'" by which practitioners realize that their practices are not working as intended and are "moved to a mode of deliberation or reflection that prompts them to ask, 'Why do unequal outcomes exist?' 'What can we do?'" (Bensimon 2007, pp. 455–456). Disaggregating data by race to reveal equity gaps can inspire practitioners to pose critical questions, dig deeper, and, after learning more, take action to close those gaps.

In her essay "The Misbegotten URM as a Data Point," Estela Bensimon (2016) critiques yet another way that institutions try to avoid disaggregating outcome data by race by using the generic designation "URM" – short for underrepresented minorities – to refer to Black, Latinx, Pacific Islander, and Native American students collectively. Often institutions with relatively low African American, Latinx, Native American, and Native Hawaiian and Pacific Islander enrollments aggregate students from these racial/ethnic categories into a single group when presenting student outcome data.

Bensimon argues that this practice undermines institutional efforts to achieve racial equity. While it might be more palatable to talk about URMs as a group instead of naming the specific inequities experienced by Black, Latinx, Native American, and Native Hawaiian and Pacific Islander students, doing so is a "form of malpractice" that "circumvents the race question" (Bensimon 2016, p. 5). Using the generic designation, URM erases the unique and complex sociopolitical, sociohistorical, and sociocultural factors that contribute to the deeply entrenched inequities experienced across racially minoritized groups, including historical and ongoing exclusionary and discriminatory policies and practices. Using the term *URM* glosses over the different manners in which African Americans, Latinxs, Native Americans, Alaska Natives, Native Hawaiians, and Pacific Islanders came to be underrepresented within higher education (Bensimon 2016).

Chapter 2 of this volume describes how the use of the term *URM* can undermine frank discussions of race and racial inequity. The euphemistic URM can also lead to mischaracterizations and misunderstandings of the actual state of racial equity on campuses. Lumping Black, Latinx, Native American, Alaska Native, Native Hawaiian, and Pacific Islander students together in a catchall category can hide significant inequities in outcomes across these groups. Figure 3.2 illustrates this phenomenon using the fictitious completion rate data from the previous example. In the example, 140 out of 400 Black students completed their degrees, corresponding to a completion rate of 35%. Five hundred out of 1,000 Latinx students completed their degree, corresponding to a completion rate of 50%. Both groups are experiencing inequities in terms of degree completion, but the equity gap experienced by Black students is far larger than that of Latinx students when comparing them to the highest-performing group. As shown in Figure 3.2, aggregating Black and Latinx students together using the generic designation URM corresponds to a completion rate of 46% (640 out of 1400 students complete their degree). Using the URM category still shows that an equity gap exists, but it masks the difference in outcomes between Black and Latinx students. It also prevents practitioners

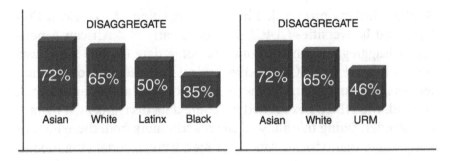

Figure 3.2   How using URM masks inequities.

from considering that the factors that contribute to the equity gaps experienced by Black and Latinx students are likely distinct in some ways.

It is important to note that while disaggregating data by race is a necessary step to advancing equity, it is also true that the institution's own context, and the broader social and historical context in which that institution is embedded, should inform the specific racial/ethnic categories used. Special mission institutions and institutions located in geographic areas with high concentrations of minoritized individuals ought to consider those factors when disaggregating data by race/ethnicity. For example, many of California's community colleges enroll a significant number of Southeast Asian (e.g., Vietnamese, Filipinx) students and always ensure that outcome data for these groups are disaggregated and not lumped in with the broader Asian category. In Minnesota, a state with relatively large Hmong and Somali populations, some institutions disaggregate outcome data for these groups along with the current racial/ethnic categories used by IPEDS (i.e., African American/Black, Hispanic/Latino, Asian, American Indian or Alaska Native, Native Hawaiian or Other Pacific Islander, white, two or more races).

When disaggregating data by race/ethnicity, minority-serving institutions may have to consider what categories make sense given the demographic makeup of their student population. The two historically Black institutions that participated in the Committing to Equity and Inclusive Excellence: Campus-Based Strategies for

Student Success project, led by the Association of American Colleges and Universities (*AAC&U*), were nearly 90% African American. Disaggregating institutional outcome data by race alone was not as helpful to HBCUs in the project because the equity challenges these institutions face were more complex and intersectional. Instead, the HBCUs examined outcome data disaggregated by race *and* gender. Doing this allowed the practitioners from these institutions to see that African American men were experiencing inequities in terms of retention and completion. Seeing the inequities in the data guided the questions that these two campus teams asked of themselves and led them to questions their own practices. From the perspective of these practitioners, failing to create equity for Black men meant that their home institution was not fully meeting its mission as outlined by the HBCU designation. In this instance, the practitioners used their knowledge of their own institutional context to guide their use of disaggregated data.

In sum, disaggregating data by race is critical to revealing inequitable outcomes. However, compiling data disaggregated by race is only a first step toward achieving equity. Equally important is the critical sensemaking process during which practitioners notice racial inequities and begin to ask themselves what they can do to close existing equity gaps. Thus, practitioners should not see disaggregated data as the end product, but as a powerful tool to advance equity.

We Have Equity Gaps ... What Now?

Current patterns of college access and completion within US higher education suggest that most institutions, after disaggregating outcome data by race/ethnicity, will find that some racially minoritized students on their campus experience educational inequities. Thus, it is important to outline how practitioners can, beginning with disaggregated data and engaging in equity-minded sensemaking, come to understand the state of equity on their campus across academic programs, divisions, and departments.

Data, like resources, are not "self-acting" (Cohen et al. 2003; Dowd and Bensimon 2015). In other words, the value of data depends on how they are used (Cohen et al. 2003). The value of disaggregated data as it relates to advancing equity depends on the ways in which practitioners contextualize and make meaning of that data. "Equity-minded sensemaking" is how CUE describes this process of critical reflection, contextualization, and meaning-making. *Equity-minded sensemaking* goes beyond examining data and noticing equity gaps in outcomes. It involves interpreting equity gaps as a signal that practices are not working as intended and asking equity-minded questions about how and why current practices are failing to serve students experiencing inequities.

Equity-minded sensemaking can be fostered among practitioners through the use of open-ended prompts to guide discussions of data disaggregated by race/ethnicity. Such prompts might include asking practitioners:

- What patterns do you notice in the data?
- Which racial groups are experiencing inequities?
- Which racial group(s) would you prioritize for goal setting, and why?
- What are your equity goals?
- What are your hunches about what might be contributing to the equity gaps?
- What additional data do you want to collect to better understand the gap?
- What equity-minded questions might you pursue with further inquiry?

The discussion resulting from the framing questions above enables practitioners to delve deeper into the equity gaps revealed by the data. Emphasizing additional data collection ensures that efforts to close equity gaps are based on evidence. Asking practitioners to generate additional equity-minded questions encourages them to remain focused on remediating practices instead of blaming students for the inequities they experience. Using data to generate questions is important because it underscores that equity gaps are tied to policies and practices that could be intentionally designed to better support the students who experience the gaps. These equity-minded questions can then be pursued through practitioner inquiry, or the study of one's own practices, with the insights gained in this process acting as a guide for institutional action and change. In this respect, examining data opens the door to examining practices.

It is important to note that equity-minded sensemaking does not involve presupposing the causes of equity gaps and jumping to solutions. Practitioners are not asked, "What would you do to solve the equity gaps?" Instead, equity-minded sensemaking aims to foster a culture of inquiry so that institutional and practitioner action is guided by evidence and directed at those practices that contribute to or exacerbate inequities.

The Importance of Data "Close to Practice"

In CUE's practitioner inquiry model, quantitative data disaggregated by race/ethnicity is the starting point to reveal where equity gaps in student outcomes exist. Institutional equity efforts continuously use quantitative measures to monitor progress in the closing of equity gaps over time. Practitioners may also collect qualitative data on their own practices and the ways in which students experience them in order to pinpoint the mechanisms by which inequities originate and persist.

When viewed with an equity-minded lens, disaggregated student outcome data can highlight where practitioners can take intentional action to reach an institution's equity goals. Imagine, for example, that the institution experiencing the completion-rate equity gaps shown in Figure 3.1 aims to better understand what it can do to eliminate the inequities. Practitioners examining the data together may then look at course completion data disaggregated by race/ethnicity in order to identify those specific departments or courses that act as barriers to equitable degree completion. After identifying a department or course in which African American or Latinx students experience equity gaps, inquiry – like course observations and syllabi reviews – can be deployed to identify the following:

- Institutional practices that are supporting student groups experiencing gaps;
- Practices that are inadvertently contributing to or failing to address inequities; and
- How some practices could be modified, reconsidered, or replaced to close the equity gaps in completion within those courses and departments.

This process of moving from high-level indicators to finer-grained quantitative measures and other qualitative data close to practice (Dowd and Bensimon 2015; Dowd et al. 2018) is central to practitioner learning and change. It enables practitioners to "find the actionable N," or where they can make changes in their own practices to improve outcomes for students with whom they interact in order to move the needle and close equity gaps (Dowd et al. 2018). The following example describes how a team of practitioners can begin with disaggregated data and engage in equity-minded sensemaking to identify how changes in practices might lead to narrowing equity gaps.

Imagine that a group of math faculty members is working collaboratively to understand the nature of inequities in course success within its department. They may begin by examining course completion data disaggregated by race (see Figure 3.3).

The faculty members examining this data observe that Asian students have the highest course completion rate (62.9%) and that Native Americans, African Americans, and Latinx students experience the largest equity gaps. They also notice that the number of additional course completions needed to close the equity gaps is largest for Latinx students – not surprising given that nearly half of students enrolling in basic skills math courses at the institution are Latinx. While these data enabled the faculty members to determine the groups experiencing inequities, they need additional data to figure out which courses contribute most to these equity gaps.

Racial/ethnic group	Number of course enrollments at census	Number of course enrollments completed successfully	Percent of course enrollments completed successfully (%)	Highest performing group's course completion rate (%)	Percentage point gap	Number of additional course completions needed to close the gap
Asian	437	275	**62.9**	62.9	—	
Black or African American	71	25	35.2	62.9	-27.7	20
Hispanic/Latinx	1237	516	41.7	62.9	-21.2	263
Native Am./ Alaska Native	14	4	28.6%	62.9	-34.3	5
Native Hawaiian/ Pacific Isl.	16	8	50.0	62.9	-12.9	3
Two or More Races	126	61	48.4	62.9	-14.5	19
Unknown	42	16	38.1	62.9	-24.8	11
White	845	523	61.9	62.9	-1.0	9
Total	**2788**	**1428**	**51.2**			

Notes: Successful course completion is defined as earning a grade of A, B, C, or P.
Success rates are computed using the duplicated enrollment count of students enrolled in more than one course in a given academic year.
The "number of additional course completions needed to close the gap" indicates the number of additional successful course completions needed by that subgroup to equal or exceed the highest performing group's course completion rate.

Figure 3.3 Basic skills mathematics course completion data disaggregated by race.

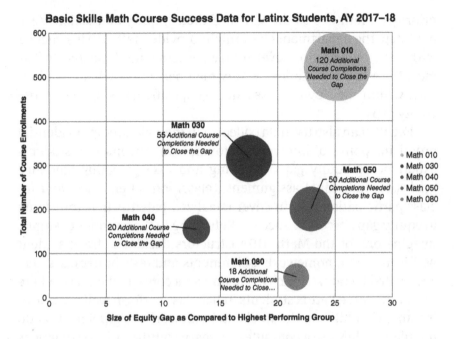

Figure 3.4   Example of course-level data to guide practitioner action.

Figure 3.4 illustrates the next round of data reviewed by the math faculty members. In the figure, the size of the equity gaps experienced by Latinx students in the five basic skills math courses are displayed, both in terms of percentage points and the number of course completions lost. Showing the data in this way allows the faculty members to quickly identify which basic skills math courses contribute the most to the inequities experienced by Latinx students. Given that both time and resources are finite, the math faculty can first focus on those courses most "at-risk," maximizing the return on their efforts.

As shown in Figure 3.4, Math 010 is the course with the highest number of course enrollments by Latinx students and it is the course for which Latinx students experience the most severe equity gap in course success, relative to the highest-performing group. This graph clearly makes the case that the math faculty ought to prioritize Math 010 as the target of their inquiry and action. As a next step, the department chair might provide Math 010 instructors with their own section-level course success data disaggregated by race. Doing so would allow faculty members to see what inequities exist within their own classes and set specific goals to close those equity gaps.

Faculty can also use data collected in their classrooms to identify promising points of intervention to improve outcomes for students experiencing equity gaps. Tracking and disaggregating students' grades on individual assignments, classroom attendance, and in-class participation may uncover racialized patterns that contribute to equity gaps in course success. Returning to the previous example, imagine one of the Math 010 instructors decides to track student performance on homework assignments and tests in her class, disaggregated by race/ethnicity. She notices a consistent pattern where two of the three Latinx students in her class perform well (i.e., earning an "A" or "B") on the weekend homework assignments that do not require they use a computer, but earn significantly lower grades (i.e., C– or lower) on those weekend assignments that require the use of a computer. Noticing this, the instructor approaches those students to ask what is going on and learns that neither has reliable access to a computer at home. To complete the homework assignments that were distributed on Friday and due the following Monday, the students had to rely on the campus computer lab, which was not open on weekends. The students explained that because the homework was due on Monday, they had to rush to complete their Math 010 homework on Friday afternoon in the two hours they had between receiving the assignment and when the computer lab closed. Due to this conversation, the instructor realizes that her assumption that the students in her class would face no obstacles accessing a computer to complete the weekend homework assignments was misguided, and that this assumption had unintentionally contributed to equity gaps in her classroom. Going forward, the Math 010 instructor decided to give all students an additional day to turn in the computer-based homework assignments. She also raised the possibility of opening the computer lab on weekends with her department chair.

The Math 010 instructor's use of "data close to practice" illustrates how everyday indicators of what is happening in the classroom can highlight where different groups experience barriers and momentum points. By examining her gradebook disaggregated by race, the Math 010 instructor was able to connect the observations represented in course-level student success data shown in Figure 3.4 to her own day-to-day practices. While the small changes she made will not close the equity gaps in Math 010 success experienced by Latinx students as a whole, the changes she made will better support student success in her classroom and advance equity.

The above example is admittedly simplistic – what leads to equity gaps is often far more complex than ensuring students have access to learning resources like a computer. The root causes of inequities vary from minoritized group to minoritized group; there is no panacea or one-size-fits-all solution. The point here is that using data in the classroom can uncover racialized patterns that occur within our classrooms and cause practitioners to think more critically about taken-for-granted assumptions that can have a disproportionately negative impact on racially minoritized students. Data close to practice provide a critical tool for identifying campus-specific and classroom-specific actions needed to realize equity.

Examining disaggregated data often sparks new ideas and raises critical questions about how faculty and other higher education practitioners can make changes to create more equitable learning environments. These questions can be pursued with practitioner research and inquiry. Faculty may review course syllabi, conduct classroom observations, or administer student surveys to understand how racially minoritized students experience the classroom and to identify actions they can take to ensure that their practices are equity-minded and adequately support success for racially minoritized students.

Putting Equity-Mindedness into Practice

The ubiquity of data in higher education's current moment is a double-edged sword. As the preceding discussion illustrates, data can be a valuable tool to advance equity at the institutional, departmental, and classroom-levels, when it is used in equity-minded ways. However, data can also be used to reinforce stereotypes and justify misguided yet deeply held beliefs about racially minoritized students. Data can reveal which student groups experience inequitable outcomes and describe the nature of those inequities. However, if practitioners fail to employ an equity-minded lens and are unwilling to see things critically, equity gaps may remain. When seeking to address equity gaps in course completion in the earlier example, the Math 010 instructor was willing to examine her own practices to determine how they might be made more inclusive to serve students equitably. For data to be effective in advancing equity, it is critical that practitioners are willing and able to (i) make sense of data in terms of practices instead of student deficits and (ii) interrogate the people, practices, and policies that lead to equity gaps.

Thinking about equity gaps made visible by disaggregated data in this way takes practice, and higher education practitioners who make sense of data in equity-minded ways may experience pushback from well-intended colleagues who instinctually apply a more deficit-minded frame. The following case study exercise presents a fictitious scenario to outline some of the challenges that practitioners may encounter when using data to advance equity. The scenario centers on a faculty meeting during which the department chair encourages her colleagues to review course completion data disaggregated by race and ethnicity. The case study reflects three common forms of pushback that we have encountered while working with higher education practitioners who are examining disaggregated data as a part of campus equity efforts. The questions following each example are intended to prompt reflection on how practitioners can navigate such resistance and redirect discussions back toward equity-minded sensemaking.

Case Study Exercise: Encouraging Equity-Minded Sensemaking

Nathalie Durand opened the first faculty meeting of the year by announcing that she would be making the review of student outcome data disaggregated by race/ethnicity and gender a regular agenda item. As the newly elected chemistry department chair, Dr. Durand wanted to do something to better understand why so few women and students of color seemed to major in chemistry at the university. She thought that by reviewing success rates for all courses taught by her department, she and her colleagues would be able to identify specific courses that acted as barriers to achieving equity in chemistry.

She passed around a handout that displayed the disaggregated data for each chemistry course. As she made her way back to the front of the room, she heard murmuring from many of her colleagues. "So," she began, trying to get the attention of the faculty, "do you want me to talk you through the data?"

The Deficit-Minded Professor

"No, I think it's pretty clear," responded Dr. Watt. "We're chemists, after all." He continued, "The outcomes for my course are right where I want them to be. About 60% of my students are passing. I don't see the issue."

Dr. Durand frowned as she looked at the success rates for Organic Chemistry, Dr. Watt's course. "Well, we can discuss why you think 60% is right where you want them to be in a minute. I wanted to ask you if you noticed that the success rate for Latinx students is 45%. And, it's not that much higher for African Americans—50% for all Black students and 33% for Black men."

(continued)

(continued)

A flash of embarrassment crossed Dr. Watt's face before he answered, "Well, I can't help that. Those students are just not prepared for the rigors of the course. I shouldn't be blamed for that." Dr. Durand began to respond, but Dr. Watt quickly cut her off.

"Anyway, all of that is beside the point. It's the overall success rate that matters – not just the rates of *some* students."

Part 1: Discussion Questions

- How should Dr. Durand respond to Dr. Watt's comment about the overall success rate being the only outcome that matters?
- How might you encourage him to reflect on the data and try to make sense of it in a critical manner?

Multivariate Thinking

"Well, we should expect some variation in outcomes," said Mark Paige, the previous department chair. "I mean, students have different backgrounds, different levels of preparation, and they vary in terms of academic ability. I would never expect that the success rate would be the same for all students."

Dr. Durand began to explain that the university was using parity in outcomes as its definition for equity, so the department needed to follow suit. As she was talking, Dr. Paige was shaking his head no vigorously.

"I'm sorry Nathalie, but O-Chem is a hard class, and it should stay that way. I don't think that Dr. Watt should lower his standards just to make sure that more African American and Hispanic students pass. Besides, I bet if we controlled for race, socioeconomic status, and whether they took AP Chem in high school, these racial differences would disappear."

Part 2: Discussion Questions

- How would you respond to Dr. Paige's contention that "we should expect some variation" in course success rates? Do you agree?
- What is problematic about Dr. Paige's suggestion to control for race/ethnicity, gender, and other student characteristics?

Data Skeptic

"Look, I'm all for reviewing data in our meetings, but it needs to be accurate," said Cynthia Moody, a professor in the department. "I've been here for 20 years, and I've never seen success rates this low for my physical chemistry course. I don't understand what changed last year. These data have to be wrong. They can't possibly be correct."

Dr. Durand responded, "Kay from the IR Office generated this for me, so I am fairly certain it's right."

Dr. Moody retorted, "Well, I don't believe it. These differences in group outcomes are not even statistically significant. I am not going to change anything in my class based on incorrect data from a single semester."

Part 3: Discussion Questions

- How would you respond to Dr. Moody?
- What additional data might you request from the institutional research office to address Dr. Moody's concerns?

Communicating Data to Advance Equity

One of the most heartening results from AAC&U's Committing to Equity and Inclusive Excellence project was the level at which participating institutions bought in to using data as a tool to advance equity. The final project report revealed that nearly all institutions took actionable steps to make disaggregated data more readily available to campus practitioners. A number of campuses created data dashboards providing easy access to data for a number of indicators of interest. These dashboards allow practitioners to explore outcome measures of interest in a disaggregated format. In tabular and/or graphic form, the dashboards enable practitioners to make monitoring data a routine practice.

To ensure that these dashboards effectively advance equity, it is important that practitioners have access to models of equity-minded data use and can receive coaching on how to use data in equity-minded ways. Offices of institutional research most commonly tasked with creating these dashboards might include a sidebar with examples of questions that can be answered with the data. Additionally, these offices should ensure the documentation they provide dashboard users shows examples of how they can use the data to explore the state of racial equity in outcomes. When feasible, it is also important to assess the frequency with which these data dashboards are used and the manner in which practitioners are using them. Doing so would allow institutions to understand whether and how dashboards promote practitioner data use as an organizational routine.

Dashboards are one of the primary ways that higher education institutions communicate data to their campus communities. Simply ensuring practitioners can access data is not enough. Equally important is the nature of the language used to talk about data and to frame the gaps that might emerge when disaggregating data by race. Characterizing disparities in outcomes as "achievement gaps" is very different from describing these disparities as "equity gaps." The term *achievement gap,* while common, is rooted in deficit thinking. It places the onus of redressing educational disparities on the very students who experience inequities because it suggests that students are failing to "achieve." The term suggests that students are solely responsible for acting, and the language sends a message that practitioners do not have to engage in critical reflection on their practices. The term *equity gap,* on the other hand, evokes the notion that institutions have a responsibility to create equity for students. If institutional leaders and practitioners use deficit-minded language when discussing equity challenges, access to data will do no good for advancing equity because such language communicates the expectation that students are expected to create equity for themselves.

Developing Institutional Capacity to Use Data in Equity-Minded Ways

The Committing to Equity and Inclusive Excellence project teams displayed a wide range of data-related institutional capacity. Some institutions had large, fully staffed institutional research (IR) offices that had long compiled and presented outcome data to campus communities. Other institutions had only recently begun to develop institutional research capacity and were not used to disaggregating outcome data by race on a regular basis.

This range in experience with using data led to an interesting pattern, whereby some project teams found the disaggregated graduation and retention rate data we asked them to discuss too simplistic, while others were concerned about the workload associated with compiling institutional data disaggregated by race. The range in IR capacity was a very real challenge that had to be confronted during the course of the project.

We explained during each project convening that, no matter the sophistication or developmental stage of an IR office, we hoped all participating institutions would come to understand how data can be used as a tool to advance equity. Instead of dwelling on the differences in institutional capacity, CUE researchers and AAC&U staff emphasized the ways in which disaggregated data can reveal inequities, spark conversations, and raise equity-minded questions that can be pursued using a variety of inquiry tools and methods. Indeed, it was clear from the project results that each institution understood the importance of investing time and resources to develop their capacity to use data in equity-minded ways.

Using Data as a Tool to Advance Equity

Examples from the Committing to Equity and Inclusive Excellence Project Teams

Data Dashboards

More than half of all Committing to Equity and Inclusive Excellence project teams reported that they either developed new or expanded existing web-accessible data dashboards. These dashboards display critical institutional indicators in a user-friendly, easy-to-understand format. The project teams created dashboards as a tool for the exploration of institutional performance on a number of metrics including student enrollment, retention, and degree completion. The dashboards are interactive, allowing members of their campus communities to easily disaggregate data, visualize equity gaps, and track these gaps over time.

As explained elsewhere in this chapter, dashboards can be an effective tool for using and communicating data to advance equity when institutions provide the scaffolding that promotes equity-minded sensemaking. Institutions that use data dashboards ought to carefully consider the language used to frame the data (e.g., "equity gap" rather than "achievement gap") and provide examples of equity-minded questions to consider after examining the data included in the dashboard.

Intersectional Approaches to Data Analysis

Several Committing to Equity and Inclusive Excellence project teams took an intersectional approach to disaggregating student outcome data. Though these teams began by disaggregating data by race, they subsequently added additional student characteristics to their analysis in order to more precisely identify those subpopulations that were experiencing the largest equity gaps. For example, two minority-serving institutions that disaggregated their outcome data by race *and* gender identified African American men as the group experiencing the largest equity gaps in terms of retention and completion. Another institution that disaggregated their data by race, gender, and age found that African American women adult learners experienced significant equity gaps. This led the team to think more deeply about how well current practices were supporting and meeting the needs of this subpopulation. An intersectional approach to data analysis can lead to valuable insights about the state of equity on campus.

Predictive Analytics

A few Committing to Equity and Inclusive Excellence project institutions opted to use predictive analytics as a tool in their equity efforts. Predictive analytics involves using multivariate statistical techniques to analyze large datasets to characterize relationships among variables in order to "predict" future behavior, events, and outcomes (Ekowo and Palmer 2016). In the context of higher education, predictive analytics often involves using past data to identify student characteristics or patterns of behavior that are associated with academic success and/or failure. These associations derived from past data can then be used to inform early warning systems and identify students who may need academic support, intrusive advising, or other interventions.

Such a tool may be helpful for promoting student success; however, there is some danger in relying too heavily on

(continued)

(continued)

predictive analytics when trying to advance equity. Generally, the unit of analysis in applications of predictive analytics within higher education is the student. Institutions aim to identify students who may struggle in the future based on the experiences and outcomes of past students. Focusing on the student in this way may de-emphasize the responsibility that institutions hold in creating racial equity. For example, predictive analytics might reveal that racially minoritized students who are placed into a certain level of freshman math are $X\%$ less likely to complete their degrees than those who do not take that course, but these statistical models cannot elucidate what it is about the math curriculum, teaching practices, or classroom climate that leads to that result. Critically reflecting on practices is central to advancing equity, and predictive analytics are not a substitute for that.

Predictive analytics can also unintentionally further educational inequity if used inappropriately or in isolation (Ekowo and Palmer 2016). If, for example, an advisor dissuades a minoritized student from a specific major based on an algorithm that predicts that student is unlikely to succeed in that degree program, equity is undermined, not advanced. Predictive analytics can be a productive tool to support institutional equity efforts. However, this approach needs to be deployed with care in a critical and equity-minded manner.

Engaging Faculty in the Examination of Data and Critical Self-Reflection

Several Committing to Equity and Inclusive Excellence project teams convened a series of workshops designed to engage faculty in equity efforts. Though the exact structure of these workshops varied from campus to campus, they shared common elements, including examining disaggregated student outcome data, providing faculty with course-level and/or section-level success data for the courses they teach, and encouraging faculty to probe their own practices to better understand how they may contribute to the equity gaps present in the data.

These workshops provided a structured opportunity for faculty to engage in equity-minded sensemaking and to plan for inquiry into their own practices. Rather than being told by others where equity gaps exist and which student groups experience them, faculty were able to uncover gaps for themselves. Similarly, enabling faculty to critically reflect on their own practices and analyze their own course syllabi promotes practitioner learning and change.

Chapter 4

Aligning Strategic Priorities and Building Institutional Capacity

Equity for Whom?

The growing use of the word *equity* in higher education has led to vague interpretations of its meaning and a lack of clarity in what goals and actions should be widely shared and commonly understood when campuses seek to elevate equity as a core institutional value. As previously mentioned in Chapters 2 and 3, the Center for Urban Education's (*CUE*) deliberate focus on racial equity challenges educators to become more equity-minded by "critically assess[ing] racialization in their own practices" and encourages educators to stop using coded language when describing minoritized students. Coded language deflects from deep conversations on how racism has shaped – and continues to shape – our systems, policies, structures, and beliefs. In other words, we must clearly identify the groups that have experienced inequities in our educational system by race and ethnicity in order to begin to investigate honestly why these inequities persist.

At the Association of American Colleges and Universities (AAC&U), we agree that a focus on equity must specifically examine racial equity because of its unique historical, sociocultural, and sociopolitical circumstances. This focus is even more relevant today because, according to the American Council on Education's report *Race and Ethnicity in Higher Education*, "In 2015–16, approximately 45 percent of all undergraduate students identified as being a race or ethnicity other than White, compared with 29.6 percent in 1995–96" (Espinosa et al. 2019, p. 43). The diversity of the undergraduate student population should make it impossible to ignore racial equity. However, we realize that for many institutions, the growing intersectionality of student identities, as well as the increasing equity divides among other defined groups, compels campus educators to examine inequities not only based on race and ethnicity, but also across gender, sexuality, socioeconomic status, age, geographic background, disability, national origin, and religion to fully serve the students that higher education institutions seek to educate in order to make excellence inclusive. When we focus on inclusive excellence, we are seeking "to uncover inequities in student success, identify effective educational practices, and build such practices organically for sustained institutional change" (AAC&U n.d.). For these reasons, we return in this chapter to a broader definition of equity because we want to meet you where you are on your equity journey, while encouraging you to examine racial equity as a primary component of your equity imperative. We recognize through our collective experiences working with educators at colleges and universities that a both/and proposition for examining multiple forms of inequities often leads to a decreased focus on racial equity because of the complexities of the conversations surrounding race and the necessary actions required to remedy racism in our deeply ingrained beliefs and practices that are part of our history and our present. As we engage in conversations focused on equity in higher education, we must remain vigilant and have higher levels of accountability to address racial equity in higher education. We must constantly self-assess and act to ensure that we are not promoting an either/or proposition in our efforts to advance equity in higher education, but a both/and definition to examine all forms of inequities, so that racial and ethnic inequities are not minimized but receive equal levels of attention that will ultimately lead to sustainable change for students.

Clarity in Language

In *America's Unmet Promise* written by scholars from the CUE and published by AAC&U (Witham et al. 2015, p. 27), the authors outlined CUE's principles for creating equity by design:

- Clarity in language, goals, and measures is vital to effective equitable practices.
- Equity-mindedness should be the guiding paradigm for language and actions.
- Equitable practices and policies are designed to accommodate differences in the contexts of students' learning – not to treat all students the same.
- Enacting equity requires a continual process of learning, disaggregating data, and questioning assumptions about relevance and effectiveness.
- Equity must be enacted as a pervasive institution and system-wide principle.

To promote the first and last principles of equity by design, most higher education institutions have mission statements or diversity, equity, and inclusion statements to indicate to internal and external constituents the campus values and goals that are core principles guiding institutional efforts to advance diversity, equity, and inclusion in support of higher levels of student learning and success. This section discusses some real-world examples, slightly modified to maintain the confidentiality of the respective institutions.

Mission Statements

- College A provides a high-quality education to ensure all students successfully complete their educational goals while developing as engaged global citizens with the life skills necessary to enrich and support themselves, their families, and their community.
- By embracing a student-centered philosophy that promotes a diverse community of learners, College B integrates instruction and student services in collaboration with industry and educational partners to empower students to be global citizens.
- College C provides opportunities for students to develop proficiency in core areas, including critical thinking, quantitative reasoning, information competency, written and oral communication, ethical reasoning, diversity, and global awareness. Student learning and personal development are supported by expansive student services programs and community partnerships.

To truly commit to and enact the values they include, statements must be widely shared and understood by internal and external constituencies. In our experience working with campuses, institutions dedicate a significant amount of time and effort to developing these statements as part of strategic planning processes, but they give little time and effort to helping campus educators, students, and external constituents understand definitions of the terms and what they mean in practice.

In the first example, how does College A define "a high-quality education" and how will the college measure that? How does College A measure progress toward ensuring "all students successfully complete their educational goals"?

In the next example, how does College B define "a student-centered philosophy"? Is this philosophy widely shared? How is it practiced?

In the third example, how does College C assess the defined learning outcomes? And how do student services programs and community partnerships support student development of these learning outcomes? Are these strategies effective?

To accomplish this, campus leaders should provide ongoing open forums for educators to raise key questions regarding how the institution defines the language used in these statements and to collaboratively develop accountability frameworks that translate the definitions into campus practice. The focus here should be on specifics and not using coded language. For example, at AAC&U, we define a high-quality education as the development of student proficiency of transparent and defined learning outcomes associated with completion of a course, program, or degree through participation in high-impact practices (HIPs), project-based learning, applied learning experiences, and the students' ability to articulate what has been learned and apply it to complex settings and unscripted problems. All of these are connected to the skills and competencies that will prepare students for lifelong and career success.

If this is how your institution defines a high-quality education, then what data does your institution collect to ascertain if it is providing a high-quality education for all students?

- Do you have defined learning outcomes for courses, programs, and degrees?
- Are the outcomes transparent for students?
- How are they assessed?
- Are the data from assessing student proficiency of learning outcomes disaggregated?
- How are the data shared? How are the data used for institutional, teaching and learning improvement efforts?
- What makes the educational practices that help students develop proficiencies in the defined learning outcomes high-impact? High-quality?
- What are your institutional metrics for measuring design quality? Are the designs tied to what research shows will help students achieve proficiency in the learning outcomes?
- How does your campus know that these learning outcomes align with workforce preparation?

This list of questions is not exhaustive, but it is included to highlight the need to clarify language that in many instances has become commonplace in higher education without being fully understood by educators responsible for achieving the goals. These are the types of questions that should be regularly discussed in ongoing campus forums, and in program and department meetings, and not regulated to once or twice a year. After the data are compiled, disaggregated, and shared, if there are inequities across student groups, then the conversation on campus should begin to ask why. The *why* conversation returns us to what it means to be an equity-minded educator and to the strategies for building a campus culture of equity-mindedness outlined in Chapter 2.

Diversity, Equity, and Inclusion Statements

Diversity, equity, and inclusion statements can easily be a vision that everyone agrees with but no one understands. These statements are often ambitious and include aspirational goals. Often, campuses do not want to address these statements critically to examine how institutional practices need to change to achieve the goals. As Eric Dey stated, we must examine "the 'real' versus the 'ideal' view of campus environments and the inconvenient truths that these views are often dissimilar" (2009, p. 11). But, what does that mean? It requires educators to not only describe the aspirational goals, as many do in these types of statements, but to deeply and honestly reflect on why these goals have not been met and what needs to change.

Below, we share three examples of college diversity, equity, and inclusion statements and reflective questions that could guide the campuses in achieving these goals.

- College D is a community that includes and values the voices of all people. As such, we recognize the social barriers that have systematically marginalized and excluded people and communities based on race, ethnicity, gender, sexual identity, socioeconomic background, age, disability, national origin, and religion. We are committed to the equity of opportunities and strive to promote and advance diverse communities. We value and proactively seek genuine participation from these historically underrepresented and underserved groups and recognize them as an essential component of creating a welcoming and rich academic, intellectual, and cultural environment for everyone.

- College E, integrates principles of diversity, access, and inclusion throughout policy, practice, services, and curriculum to close equity gaps in student outcomes and create an equitable work environment.
- At College F, diversity is an invitation to celebrate the uniqueness of each individual, as well as the cultural differences that enrich us all. College F strives to ensure that individuals from all backgrounds and perspectives are served equitably. The diversity that students, staff, and faculty bring is viewed as a resource, strength, and benefit to the college as a whole. In a world that is multicultural and ever-changing, College F fosters a campus climate that is respectful and inclusive of the many identities of our community members in terms of gender, sexual orientation, disability, age, socioeconomic status, ethnicity, race, culture, perspective, and other background characteristics. We commit to incorporating diversity and equity into our hiring practices, student and staff recruitment, curricular and cocurricular activities, and daily functions at the college. College F is committed to affirming and protecting the dignity and rights of each person and addressing issues of bias, discrimination, and exclusion where they exist. We celebrate and value the diversity and strive to promote an inclusive community that is welcoming and supporting of all.

Analyzing the diversity, equity, and inclusion statements also prompts questions for further investigation. In the first example, who are the underrepresented and underserved groups? When we use this type of language without taking the next step of specifically naming who these students are, we are using the racially coded language described in Chapter 2. Why are the underrepresented and underserved students designated as the "other" through the use of the word *them* in this statement? Has the institution taken time to examine the social barriers that perpetuate marginalization and exclusion? Are there places on campus where these social barriers also exist? How does the institution know that it is providing equity in opportunities? What are accountability metrics for this statement?

In the next example, College E, define and measure diversity, access, and inclusion to ensure that it is integrated "throughout policy, practice, services, and curriculum to close equity gaps in student outcomes and create an equitable work environment." What is an equitable work environment? Does this exist at the institution?

For College F, what are strategies and accountability metrics for ensuring "that individuals from all backgrounds and perspectives are served equitably"? What can be learned from a campus climate survey to ascertain if "the diversity that students, staff, and faculty bring to the college are viewed as a resource, strength, and benefit to the college as a whole?" How is it transparent that the institution is committed to incorporating "diversity and equity into our hiring practices, student and staff recruitment, curricular and cocurricular activities, and daily functions at the college?"

At AAC&U, we advocate for using the term underserved as institutions initially engage in discussions for engaging in equity-focused efforts, because it requires institutions to reframe their conversations to take responsibility for better serving the students who fall into this category and not to predetermine through preconceived notions and viewpoints who these students are or might be. Any student can be underserved, depending on the institutional environment. It is our responsibility as educators to ensure students are better served and better educated. For campus educators to examine equity, they must name who the students are who fall into this category by race, ethnicity, gender, sexuality, disability, age, or other demographic groups. By specifically naming the students who fall into the underserved category, educators can't ignore that there are differences by student demographics and should engage in the difficult conversations of exploring why these exist. We must remember that defining who is underserved is not the final destination. This means acknowledging and examining the systems, structures, and personal beliefs that perpetuate racism and other prejudices such as sexism, ableism, or ageism. There are several key questions to consider when examining how to better serve students:

- What are we doing as educators to contribute to students not achieving equitable outcomes?
- How are our policies, practices, or procedures creating barriers for student success?
- How can we better serve our students by changing our actions, challenging our beliefs, or addressing our perceived notions and stereotypes?

These are questions that educators at colleges and universities should ask and answer prior to any efforts to commit to equity and inclusive excellence to ensure that there is clarity in language, goals, and measures and that those viewpoints and values are widely shared and understood.

Discussing Definitions of Equity

Most of the institutions in AAC&U's Committing to Equity and Inclusive Excellence project were able to connect their institution's mission or diversity, equity, and inclusion statements with the goals of the project to demonstrate the alignment of priorities. However, we quickly learned as a community of practice that the existence of the language doesn't mean that there is wide understanding of what the terminology means in practice. After the institutions completed the Equity Academy (as described in Chapter 1) and returned to their respective institutions to start implementing their action plans, they quickly realized that some of the language, goals, and actions they used to examine equity were not widely understood. Campus team leaders for Lansing Community College (*LCC*) acknowledged this lack of clarity:

> We realized that we had made three basic, but major, oversights in our equity and inclusion work at LCC: we did not have a common

definition of equity or understanding of equity across the college; while we could identify many potential solutions for the equity gaps, without applying multiple perspectives to definitions of equity, we were missing a collaboratively defined problem statement; and without a shared problem statement, we could not define our needs.

(Heutsche and Hicks 2018, p. 34)

The setbacks experienced by LCC are not unique from the experiences at other institutions initiating efforts to examine equity. As we have previously stated in this chapter, it is important for institutions to engage in dialogues to define equity, equality, diversity, and inclusion before launching any equity projects.

Campus educators should reflect on the following questions prior to engaging in efforts to address equity:

- How do we as an institution define equity?
- How is this viewpoint/definition reflected in our institutional values as stated in our mission statement or diversity, equity, and inclusion statements and evidenced in our practices?
- What language in our current mission and diversity, equity, and inclusion statements needs further clarification and to be widely shared?
- How does the institution define diversity and inclusion? How do these terms intersect with the definition of equity?
- Is the campus culture a culture of equality or a campus culture of equity? Is it both? If so, how do they intersect?
- In what ways are we addressing racial equity? What are the barriers keeping us from engaging in deep dialogue on race and racism? Are we ready to explore honestly why inequities exist?

Are Your Goals My Goals?

One of the principles for equity by design stated in *America's Unmet Promise* is that "equity must be enacted as a pervasive institution and system-wide principle" (Witham et al. 2015, p. 27). For equity initiatives to have the foundation for success, they need to be aligned with strategic priorities and other institutional initiatives. Success also depends on authentic institutional partnerships across offices and departments that are aligned with common goals, collaboration across action items, and shared accountability. In their unpublished project reports, campus teams participating in AAC&U's Committing to Equity and Inclusive Excellence project reflected that strategic alignment was necessary for their efforts to be successful:

- We realized the immediate need to revise our strategic planning work to include the overt and intentional discussion of equity. The importance of linking the Committing to Equity and Inclusive Excellence project with other related college [projects] has been transformational. From the beginning of this journey, the president and vice presidents made it clear that this work was different in that the campus culture was undergoing a transformation from its traditional focus on access to a broader focus on access and completion of credentials of value in the labor market, strongly rooted in equity.
- The university is actively engaged in a career pathways effort that teamed up with the Equity Project. The program is serving as an accelerant for career development skills, stackable credentials, and ePortfolios that encourage personal reflection and student ownership of their learning journey. Career pathways support the overall performance of our Office of Career and Professional Development and increase the connections between campus career services, faculty mentorship, and employers to help students secure job placements upon graduation. The project enables the institution to increase the number of graduates who are prepared to immediately transition to meaningful jobs and careers.
- [The] role of leadership, campus-wide partnerships, alignment with institutional goals, and professional development are success factors identified by the leadership team. Support of project initiatives by the provost, deans, and chairs and leadership team from AAC&U made it possible to acquire buy-in from

members of the faculty, students, and administrators. Support of administrators also made it easy to align project goals with those of the university. The Office of Assessment, Office of Institutional Research, Enrollment Management, Office of Student Success and Retention, and Career Development all collaborated and shared how elements of their strategic plans align with initiatives of this project. In summary, it takes the whole campus to address different dimensions of equity and inclusive excellence.

• Strategies such as aligning project goals with strategic goals and mission of the university, collaborating with different units on campus, and integrating equity and inclusive excellence strategies with the work of the general education and professional development committees are the first set of strategies for sustaining the acquired momentum and improving the culture of inclusive excellence.

When strategic goals and equity goals align, the foundation for sustainable change exists. When educators clearly understand that equity work is not separate from institutional priorities and that institutional leaders and key influencers are committed to equity, higher levels of engagement usually follow.

From these reflections, there are three key takeaways for campuses interested in engaging with equity-focused efforts:

1. Leadership support matters and is necessary for success and accountability. It must be visible and stated often.
2. Equity work cannot be done by a select few. Equity work requires collaboration and engagement across the entire institution.
3. Align equity work with the goals of other campus and system initiatives that share common goals.

When strategic goals and equity goals do not align, it results in confusion and institutional efforts that are at cross-purposes. For the equity work to move forward, several participating institutions needed leadership changes and public recognition of the value of the work. It is never enough for the mission statements and the diversity, equity, and inclusion statements to be the sole justification for why equity work is important and necessary. It must be publicly stated, repeated regularly, and aligned with institutional priorities. That alignment cannot be implicit. It must be explicit for all to see and to engage with on a regular basis.

Leveraging Resources

One of the key learning outcomes from the Committing to Equity and Inclusive Excellence project is the ongoing importance of dedicated resources for sustainability and continued success, including financial support, personnel, and coordinated campus efforts across areas of responsibilities. For example, each campus had to assess their institutional capacity to advance the shared goals of the project to increase:

- Access to and participation in HIPs
- Completion, retention, and graduation rates for low-income students, first-generation students, adult learners, and minoritized students
- Achievement of learning outcomes for underserved students using direct assessment measures
- Student awareness and understanding of the value of guided learning pathways that incorporate HIPs for workforce preparation and engaged citizenship

In their project reports, the campuses realized that higher levels of intentionality in their educational designs needed to be in place in order to ensure equitable access to learning experiences and to identify the areas of need for specific student populations:

- To increase student access to and participation in HIPs, it was significant to introduce newly developed courses for first-year students that focused on service learning, group learning elements, culturally responsive pedagogy, and current event issues in today's world. An unanticipated learning [outcome] was the development of a deeper understanding that . . . students needed more support than just traditional marketing practices to take advantage of HIP experiences and courses. Students needed structured mentoring and coaching from caring adults to help build their self-efficacy skills and sense of belonging to visualize success.

- We know that if students have advising that helps them reflect on the university's learning goals and how they apply to their individual interests, they can begin to plan how to succeed from their very first weeks on campus. With a Guided Pathways program that integrates the university's career development protocol, students know what resources are available and plan to take advantage of them to improve their chances of completion and launching their careers.

Campus educators also acknowledged that sharing disaggregated data on student outcomes provided an opportunity for faculty reflection and engagement with questions related to equity in student achievement and success. As discussed in Chapter 3, gathering and analyzing disaggregated data represent a crucial first step, but it is the process for making sense of the data from an equity-minded approach that leads to sustainable change.

- Disaggregating data by race and ethnicity to identify the classes in the first year that we need to target made it even more clear to us that our student success problem is actually an equity problem that we need to address with broad institutional and cultural changes. Working with faculty to make those changes from the ground up, beginning with pedagogy and curriculum, will continue to pay off in equity improvements.
- When grades for the courses were disaggregated by race/ethnicity, it was found that students of color were separated from white students by nearly one-half of a letter grade. This information heightened awareness and commitment of faculty teaching

these courses to take a deep dive of factors that impede better outcomes for students of color.

- We were able to triangulate various data sources to document equity gaps in STEM and use this information to raise faculty awareness, working with them to work toward pedagogical change. While we expected to take some steps forward with respect to data collection, we were pleasantly surprised to see the degree of faculty interest in addressing the equity gaps.

However, as we mentioned earlier in the book, opportunities to fully explore the complexities of what it means to be an equity-minded practitioner may not have been realized with all of the campus participants. As stated in *America's Unmet Promise*:

> Equity-minded individuals are aware of the sociohistorical context of exclusionary practices and racism in higher education and the effect of power asymmetries on outcomes for students of color and students of low socioeconomic status. Being equity-minded thus involves being conscious of the ways that higher education – through its practices, policies, expectations, and unspoken rules – places responsibility for student success on the very groups that have experienced marginalization, rather than on the individuals and institutions whose responsibility it is to remedy that marginalization.
>
> (Witham et al. 2015, p. 2)

Many of the campus teams approached this level of equity-mindedness, but deeper levels of discussions as to why the inequities exist based on structural racism, preconceived notions, and biases would have advanced their development as equity-minded practitioners. This observation reiterates the importance of ongoing engagement with equity work and that change happens in stages and learning is continuous. This point is evident in a reflection by a campus educator who was working with faculty on inclusive pedagogy:

In fall 2016 under the auspices of this grant, the institution launched Equity Resource Teams in five high-enrolled, low-success courses. The faculty involved in this cohort identified multiple high-impact, inclusive pedagogical strategies focused on eradicating achievement gaps within those courses. Beginning fall 2017, nine more high-enrolled, low-success courses were identified. The fall 2017 cohort followed a different structure as a result of lessons learned from the first cohort. With the first cohort, we asked faculty to do significant discovery through research of best practices for inclusive pedagogy. This caused some frustration. Mid-semester, we delivered some examples of key strategies for inclusive teaching that have been used nationwide. Upon our delivery of these strategies and key articles, the faculty members were relieved and were quickly able to identify some promising practices for their courses. As a result of this experience, we learned that we needed to provide more structure up-front and offer a sampling of examples at the beginning to stimulate discussion, while also still encouraging research, new ideas, and innovation. We also learned from this process that there is a necessity to build in planning for how to reach adjunct faculty if courses change.

Transparent communication related to equity goals resulted in higher levels of engagement not only by faculty, but also by staff, administrators, and students. Campuses need to ensure that mechanisms are in place for sharing data, open dialogues, deep reflection, and designing action steps for achieving equity goals. Several campuses reflected on these structures in their unpublished project reports:

- We learned the importance of strategic communication to promote transparency and create "buy-in" from faculty, staff, and administrators to support equity and inclusion work. We also learned that students play a pivotal and leading role in advancing equity and inclusion work. The students' engagement with faculty and staff through the telling of their campus experiences served as a catalyst to campus-wide action.

- We learned that when we show results to faculty, staff, administrators, and students, all constituent groups are more interested in making the changes needed to help students succeed. We also learned that when faculty, staff, administrators, and students have input into the design and procedures for continuous improvement, the project improves and becomes more institutionalized.
- We learned a lot about the power of working with faculty to make institutional change by being explicit about applying an equity-minded framework to work in the classroom, in the lab, and in department and committee meetings. Just as higher education needs to begin to acknowledge and capitalize on the strengths our students bring to college, we learned that applying the same asset-based lens to professional development with faculty is a powerful way to make change. Specifically, faculty were given agency to identify and solve equity problems in their own classes without being told by administration what the problem was and how to solve it.

To achieve transparency through strategic communication, campus leaders should consider the following questions:

- What are strategies for sharing disaggregated data on student outcomes that can engage faculty, staff, administrators, and students in equity-minded analysis, reflection, and action?
- How can we promote transparent communication strategies to encourage higher levels of engagement with equity goals and efforts?
- How can we intentionally design educational pathways that will eliminate inequities in student access?

Recommendations for Sustaining Equity Progress

When an institution has made progress toward reducing or eliminating equity gaps and campus educators are becoming more equity-minded, it is critical to engage in conversations to identify strategies to sustain the work. From our experiences, equity efforts are often project-driven and dependent on a small group of campus advocates. That is why we have emphasized the importance of leadership support that is visible, with clear goals that are communicated often to campus educators, and with dedicated resources.

Campus leaders from the Committing to Equity and Inclusive Excellence project offered recommendations on key areas to consider when developing sustainability plans:

Address initiative fatigue.

- We also . . . realized that in order to decrease the notion of initiative fatigue, it was vital to continually emphasize how this project was an important catalyst for culture change.

Provide substantive professional development opportunities to continue the transition to equity-minded practitioners.

- Provide the opportunity for faculty cohorts to participate in yearlong professional development programs that incorporate weekly online activities emphasizing equity, student success, and academic excellence.
- [Faculty development efforts should seek to] ensure that . . . course content is inclusive of a diverse set of identities.
- Institutions need to incentivize faculty to address difficult work in the classroom. Initially, less than half addressed equity-minded practices, two years later, after restructuring incentives and providing additional training, most of projects included equity-minded practices.

Maintain teams functioning across campus to scale and sustain equity progress, so the responsibility doesn't become the work of one person.

- Collaboration with other offices worked. Bringing in more minds to create and offer the programming worked. The two project components that we made less progress on were assigned to individuals. We will continue working on those two components in 2018–2019, but will use a team-based approach rather than assigning a single faculty member to lead the project. What worked were those projects clearly delineated with set expectations and goals. Less successful were those that lacked specific directions and clear reporting requirements.

- Establishment of an equity and inclusion grassroots, cross-campus representation committee of faculty, staff, administration, and students.

As we discussed above, sustainability is dependent on dedicated resources, including personnel and institutional resources that will continue to support equity goals and provide accountability structures.

- The president and vice presidents are constantly challenged with reallocating and leveraging significant resources each year to fund strategic priorities that will support large-scale reforms over the next several years. The focus and intentionality of this project helped the college lay the groundwork for strategic priorities now guiding budgetary decisions. Recommendations identified in the strategic planning process are confirmed by leadership to be priorities for implementation and converted to specific activities to form the yearly college plan. Activities also dictate funding priorities. Reallocation of existing budgets plays a key role in funding solutions. As part of the budget development process, college leadership evaluates vacant positions and identifies positions and funds to reallocate toward high-priority strategic initiatives. As a result, the college has been able to fund student completion and equity initiatives in support of strategic goals and invest in faculty and staff development. Significant resources have been reallocated over the past several years to support planning and implementation of strategic initiatives designed to transform the student experience, and we have now reached the critical point in time where these will go live for students in the fall – over $2 million has been reallocated to make these changes.
- One of the important ways in which we have leveraged resources to sustain and scale the work of this project is through collaboration with other similar projects to continue the work of data

centralization, disaggregation, and peer support networking. The University's clearly articulated priorities and alignment of budget with those priorities shared with this grant: student success and inclusive excellence will also help us leverage those resources. Assessment of HIPs learning outcomes and peer support will provide evidence for continued resource allocations. The Center for Teaching and Learning has already continued to sustain faculty and professional learning communities that are similarly focused as the ones funded by this grant.

- Perhaps the most important lesson learned and opportunity to inform future work came out of the development of our Office of Inclusion, Equity, and Diversity, newly named the Office of Inclusive Excellence. The university has also developed global goals for student success and faculty hiring. The key lessons will be the ways in which data are collected, disaggregated, analyzed, and disseminated.

- Creation of the Office of Institutional Effectiveness to assist in establishing a Student Success Scorecard (dashboards) to provide disaggregated data on student access, retention, institutional receptivity, and excellence.

- The campus is creating a new unit within Academic Affairs that will be led by a new Associate Vice President of Student Success. The current Office of Student Success Innovations and a number of other offices will be housed within this new unit. The unit will be focused on continuing the grant work and our other equity efforts.

Changing Institutional Culture

As we stated at the beginning of this chapter, the growing use of the word *equity* in higher education has led to vague interpretations of its meaning and a lack of clarity in widely shared and commonly understood goals and action when campuses seek to elevate equity as a core institutional value. Truly understanding the impact of this requires deep reflection and the ability to engage when there may be no clear pathway to success. The campuses that participated in this project took the necessary time to reflect upon the change process and to identify areas of opportunities for continued growth:

- A significant change in how we look at, talk about, and consider data is well under way. Equity is a known value at the college. Curricular changes are taking place and faculty and staff are interacting with one another for the enhancement of student success at a higher level than ever before. The culture, in short, has changed into one that is data-centric and also committed to equity.
- The most remarkable accomplishment of our project was the ability to move the college's focus on compositional diversity to collecting and examining data that provided definitive proof of the equity gaps. Discussion, dialogue, and action increased exponentially using data to fuel committed equity and inclusion work. Yet we know there is still so much more to be accomplished!
- This work has to belong to all the stakeholders and involves a tremendous amount of hard work and that the journey to secure equity will be long and difficult, but it is worth the work. That in order to secure equity and inclusiveness on our campuses, we need to belong to each other and engage in the beloved community.

Institutional change efforts are not easy to initiate, scale, or sustain. When educators engage with an effort that seeks to address systemic structures, policies, practices, and beliefs that challenge inequities and the reasons why inequities exist, the work becomes even more difficult. There are no simple answers and no linear pathways to success. The examples included in this chapter embraced various elements of what it means to move from equity talk to equity walk. As one campus team leader expressed,

I think the greatest accomplishment has been a shift in the culture from "Can't Do" to "Can Do" – in relation to faculty, staff, and students. This has been possible through an alignment of priorities and a deployment of multiple programs and across divisions to attain system and campus goals. There really has been adoption of a common language (e.g., inclusive excellence, equity) and expectations re: data as well as the adoption of a student success "ecosystem." . . . There really is a shift from what individuals can't do to change the system and what they can do. And the assumption is no longer that certain students "can't do" but rather towards what the institution "can do" to facilitate student achievement.

This reflection reinforces the belief that equity work must be constant, honest, forgiving, reflective, and brave.

This chapter highlighted institutional work that aligns with what it means to make excellence inclusive by uncovering inequities in student success, identifying effective educational practices, and building such practices organically for sustained institutional change (AAC&U n.d.). However, as we have mentioned throughout the book, the definition of equity is multidimensional, and focusing solely on the interpretation of equity from a perspective of making excellence inclusive represents an either/or approach to equity and not a both/and approach. What is missing in this part of the process is the examination of racialization in institutional practices, policies, and structures. Without that component, educators are not being equity-minded, and the transition from equity talk to equity walk is incomplete. In the next chapter, we will discuss strategies for building and assessing equity-minded competence among practitioners and leaders, with a focus on the importance of building capacity for equity-mindedness among first-generation equity practitioners.

Chapter 5

Building Capacity for Equity-Mindedness among First-Generation Equity Practitioners

Developing a Practice of Equity

In Chapter 2, we described racial equity as a project with three aims:

1. Correct the educational injustices perpetrated by policies and practices that resulted in the systematic marginalization of populations whose ties to the United States came about involuntarily through enslavement, colonization, usurpation of territory, or genocide.
2. Elevate antiracism as an agenda that higher education must take on if we are ever to truly be the just and good society we imagine ourselves to be.
3. Make whiteness be seen as the problem that undermines higher education from serving as a societal model for racial justice.

That chapter also described 10 obstacles that threaten the pursuit of these three aims, and we introduced strategies to counteract the passive and overt forms of resistance that are employed to undermine racial equity as a legitimate institutional purpose.

In this chapter, we consider how higher education leaders, administrators, faculty, staff, and trustees can acquire a practice centered on the pursuit of racial equity. We use the term *practice* to describe the way individuals do their work, the knowledge they draw on, what they judge as the right thing to do, and what they value. Practice is informed by culturally acquired knowledge that is mostly below consciousness (Polkinghorne 2004). Practice is also a reflection of disciplinary norms and beliefs. Institutional researchers may have learned to see their work as technical – for example, as they produce data reports requested by others, socialization processes may teach them that it is not their role to call attention to equity issues within the reports. In this chapter, we suggest that the practices that mediate the work of higher education professionals are not conducive to racial equity and must be remediated (Witham and Bensimon 2012).

To develop a race-conscious higher education practice, leaders, administrators, faculty, staff, and trustees need to understand whiteness to unlearn it.

Whiteness as a Practice

In Chapter 2, we pointed to whiteness as a pervasive condition of higher education that determines, albeit mostly invisibly, the processes by which things get done (e.g., the selection of students and faculty; how newcomers are socialized; the behaviors that represent adherence to core academic values, such as collegiality, professionalism, civil discourse, or good citizenship; and the criteria that drive judgments of merit, productivity, and leadership). Whiteness is evident in the deficit perspectives that practitioners draw on to explain racial inequity in educational outcomes within their institutions and classrooms. Ruth Frankenberg (1993) defines whiteness as a "set of linked dimensions" (p. 1) as follows:

1. *Whiteness is a location of structural advantage, of race privilege.*
2. *Whiteness is a "standpoint," a place from which white people look at themselves, at others, and at society.*
3. *Whiteness refers to a set of cultural practices that are usually unmarked and unnamed.*

Whiteness can be detected as the interpretive lens through which practitioners explain racialized patterns in the following ways:

- *Reiterating racialized tropes to explain lower rates of success* among racially minoritized students such as, "They don't know how to be college students," "They don't know how to study," "They sit in the back of the classroom and don't participate," "They never come for extra help," or "They don't go to the tutoring center."
- *Making unsubstantiated accusations of minoritized college students* gaming the system to profit from financial aid. We have heard this racist attribution in open-access colleges located in low-income and segregated metropolitan areas as the explanation for large dropout rates among racially minoritized students after the first few weeks of class.
- *Reaffirming debunked theories* of learning, intelligence, and cultural predispositions to justify racial inequality in education outcomes.

Below, we provide two excerpts reflecting racist perspectives on inequality expressed by white practitioners. The first relies on cultural differences to explain inequality in transfer rates at a community college and the second naturalizes inequality by bringing forth the racist scientism of genetic inferiority.

Using Cultural Predisposition as a Rationale for Racial Inequality

What I think [these data inform] me is that there might be some cultural differences in the goals of students. ... It's possible that some students have different goals based on their culture. For example, we might assume that Latino and African American students come here, perhaps, to improve their academic skills but not get a degree. Whereas there is a cultural bias in Asians to get a degree. Is that the kind of thinking that you get from this? For example, 4 out of 10 Asians are behaving as if they want to get a degree and transfer where only 1 out of 4 African Americans are (Bensimon and Harris 2012).

Using Genetic Differences as the Cause of Racial Inequality

Research shows that instructor, instruction, and educational process in the classroom affect 25% of the student outcome; 50% comes from who they are including genetics; and the remaining 25% depend on socioeconomic status of the students. This means that some students are doomed to failure when they come in. They have no motivation to succeed and they have no background in the first place. Faculty members affect such a small amount (Bustillos et al. 2011).

The ways in which problems are framed influence the solutions that practitioners can envision. W. E. B. Du Bois observed that the question whites often ask without doing so directly is, "How does it feel to be a problem?" (Du Bois [1903] 1994). More than 100 years have passed since Du Bois remarked about white peoples' perceptions of Black people as the problem; nevertheless, racial inequality continues to be framed as a problem created by minoritized populations. Code words such as *achievement gap, disadvantaged, unprivileged, underperforming, first-generation,* and *at risk* brand racially minoritized students as problems that are expected to be solved by special compensatory and remedial interventions to make the students fit into a higher education system that is responsive to and rewards whiteness. (See Obstacle 3 in Chapter 2.)

What if we appropriate the question that Du Bois discerned in the comments that whites made about race and reformulate it, constructively, to help higher education practitioners reflect on their practice and – critically – to help higher education practitioners and leaders acquire lenses to see racial inequity as a problem created and sustained by whiteness? The questions that follow can help practitioners define racial inequality as a problem created by whiteness and visible as a characteristic of its practices and mindsets:

- How does it feel to know that my practices, or those of my institution, are disadvantaging racially minoritized students?
- How does it feel to see data semester after semester that show racially minoritized students are having a deficient experience in my class or at my institution?
- How does it feel to know that I don't know how to be successful with racially minoritized students?

In asking these questions, our motivation is not to shame or imply ineptitude. We believe that higher education professionals want "to do the good" (Dowd and Bensimon 2015) but may not know what constitutes "doing the good" for racially minoritized students, mainly because they have not been taught how to do it. Racial literacy is not a required qualification for higher education practitioners, and while questions such as "How can we improve retention rates?" or "How can we increase on-time graduation?" are ubiquitous in higher education, racially conscious questions like the three posed above are not. Moreover, the reward systems of colleges and universities do not consider the production of racial equity in educational outcomes as a measure of professional excellence. Faculty members are not rewarded specifically for taking the role of institutional agents and opening opportunities for racially minoritized students (Bensimon et al. 2019). Student support service professionals may not be in the habit of routinely gathering data to learn how racially minoritized students experience the tutoring center, the library, the transfer center, or the financial aid office. Other than large-scale racial climate surveys, most institutions of higher education lack processes to inquire into the quality of the academic experience of minoritized students. The question, "In what ways do our resources work for racially minoritized students?" is not asked because it is assumed that everything an institution offers benefits "all" students as long as they have the motivation to take advantage of them. Institutions of higher education engage in program reviews, accreditation self-studies, and all kinds of evaluations, but these activities typically do not ask the race question: In what ways does whiteness operate in our practices and policies, and what is the price it imposes on racially minoritized students?

The "whiteness question" is not asked because racial equity is not considered a standard of quality, performance, or accountability. The Center for Urban Education's institutional transformation model, which is grounded in methods of critical action research, addresses the "whiteness question" by creating activity settings (Engeström 2001) purposefully designed to involve practitioners in the examination of racialization in their everyday practices, routines, and habits (Dowd and Bensimon 2015; Bensimon 2007; Peña 2012). In the next section, we draw on two decades of experience at the Center for Urban Education (*CUE*) developing tools and methods of critical action research in order to help practitioners become race-conscious and to offer a pragmatic change agenda as a way out of the hopelessness and helplessness created by explanations of racial inequity that make racially minoritized students the problem.

Educating First-Generation Equity Practitioners

In a note to Bensimon, Professor James Gray said that the phrase "first-generation equity practitioner" popped into his head as he listened to the unrehearsed talk (Perakyla 2005; Bensimon et al. 2004) of practitioners as they reviewed data on student outcomes by race and ethnicity. The practitioners' interpretation of racialized data patterns led them to the conclusion that "first-generation students need help navigating higher education [because] it's not like they can go home and ask their parents for help." Gray found their "first-gen" language aggravating. The label was being used as a substitute to evade straight talk about the black, Latinx, and Native American students whose outcomes were depicted in the data being reviewed. Even worse, the outcomes of these students were generalized as pathologies of racially minoritized students without ever naming them. "Inherent in their language were beliefs about racial hierarchies and White supremacy," Gray wrote. Thus, Gray came up with the term "first-generation equity practitioner." The difference between first-generation practitioners and students is that being branded a "first-generation equity practitioner" does not have the same stigma or consequences it does for minoritized students. As Gray explained in a memo to Estela Bensimon:

> First-generation equity practitioner was a 'political shot' to make the point that the things my family cannot help me navigate do not result in harm to me [as a white male]; that is, my mother could not help me navigate why racial inequities exist, and yet I do not have to bear the burden of other people's labels that make my deficiencies my primary identity.

We should also add that Gray and other first-generation equity practitioners will not suffer loss of compensation, poor evaluations, or mandatory remediation to become racially literate and overcome their status as first-generation equity practitioners. Their effectiveness will not be judged on the ability to help minoritized students be successful. They will not be made to feel they lack the knowledge that is expected of them. Unlike first-generation students, who are often placed in remedial education courses that don't count toward their degree, first-generation equity practitioners will not be required to spend years in pre-tenure remediation before they can move up to the real tenure track. In sum, being a first-generation equity practitioner is not stigmatizing and is not a barrier toward being tenured and promoted. The Center for Urban Education's combined experiences with thousands of higher education practitioners, particularly faculty, make clear that the majority have a strong professional identity that drives their desire to improve students' learning and lives. However, to develop into equity-minded practitioners, they need structured opportunities to remake their practice, which we address in the next section.

How First-Generation Equity Practitioners Can Become Equity-Minded

Equity-mindedness does not come naturally. It requires a knowledge base, and it takes a lot of practice. We view racial inequity as evidence that practitioners lack important knowledge. Practitioners in higher education are mostly white and have not been given the opportunity to become educated or trained to be agents of racial equity. We have observed that even among practitioners and leaders genuinely interested in achieving equity, they do and say things that are characteristic of "equity novices." It should also not be assumed that practitioners who are themselves members of minoritized groups are naturally experts in racial equity. Minoritized faculty and leaders have been socialized in the same ways as their white colleagues and therefore may also be blind to how their departments and institutions overlook the racial implications of activities and processes that appear to be race-less.

We have witnessed practitioners, predominantly those who are white, make changes in their practices after discovering that the outcomes for their courses show that the educational experiences of black, Latinx, Native American, and Pacific Islander students are qualitatively different from those of white students and sometimes Asian American students. As an example, Gray came to the concept of "first-generation equity practitioner" after participating in the Equity Scorecard team at the Community College of Aurora. Like many faculty, he was committed to student success. Equity, though, was not in his vocabulary. He acknowledges that he never considered looking at math data by race and ethnicity. But when he reviewed outcomes by course and instructor that were broken down by race and ethnicity, he saw that some faculty members were successful and some were not. The gaps between racially minoritized students and whites were as large as 35 percentage points. He also saw that his own outcomes were not very good. With the assistance of CUE's tools for equity-minded practice and through the methods of critical action research (Kemmis and McTaggart 2000; Bensimon 2007, 2012; Dowd and Bensimon 2015), Gray and his colleagues in the math department examined their data to identify racialized patterns in outcomes. They studied their syllabi to assess if their tone was welcoming and if they demystified how to be a successful math student, provided information about resources, and were respectful of students. They observed each other's classrooms to understand the quality of instructors' interactions with white students versus those with minoritized students. As the math department chair, Gray was able to develop a new and critical awareness among the mathematics faculty that brought about concrete changes in practice and major changes in outcomes. For example, success rates in intermediate algebra for black students increased by nearly 20 percentage points (from 57.5% to 77.0%) and Latinx students experienced a jump of more than 10 percentage points (69.6–80.6%). James and his colleagues attributed the improved outcomes to paying closer attention to black and Latinx students, being intentional about establishing relationships of care and respect, and – most of all – learning to ask the question, "Why is it that my teaching practices create a successful experience for white students but not for racially minoritized students?"

Gray drew on what he learned to create *Equity by Design: A Worked Example for Embedding Equity-Minded Practice into the First Three Weeks of Class* (Gray, n.d). In the tradition of CUE's engagement of practitioners as researchers of their own practices, *Equity by Design* is a tool to mediate instructors learning how to establish an equity-minded classroom culture. The tool advises practitioners that establishing an equity-minded classroom "requires deliberate, explicit, and consistent reinforcement of classroom norms and routines, which includes the regular collection of race-conscious, close-to-practice data (Dowd et al. 2018). In an email, Professor Alicia Dowd, who served as co-director of CUE for several years before joining the Pennsylvania State University as professor and director of the Center for the Study of Higher Education, explained the meaning and importance of "close-to-practice data" as follows:

> First, when accountability data are fine-grained and disaggregated by race and ethnicity, [they enable] inquiry about racial inequities to take place at a level close to educational practices under the authority and influence of participants. Access to data that [are] close to an organizational actor's own level of practice is necessary to enable organizational insiders to discover critical disturbances ... that they can remediate through their own practices.

The power of close-to-practice data is illustrated in a video made for CUE by Jason Burke, a professor at the Community College of Denver, who participated in CUE's "Math Equity" project that took place in Colorado community colleges.[1] Burke said that for a long time, he knew that his success rate in college algebra was 65% and had never looked at his data by race and ethnicity until he became involved in CUE's Math Equity project. In that project, he received data for his courses broken down by race and ethnicity, which showed that the 65% success rate was primarily due to the high performance of white students, which was 80%. In contrast, the success rate for Latinx students was 33%. Burke admits that he had not been aware of the disparity, that he had never even thought to ask for disaggregated data, and that the notion of looking at course-level data by race and ethnicity was

---

[1] The Math Equity project was jointly funded by the Teagle Foundation and the Bill and Melinda Gates Foundation. Additional information on this project is available at https://cue.usc.edu/research/colorado-equity-in-excellence.

never a consideration at the department level. In the language of CUE's theory of change (Dowd and Bensimon 2015), the juxtaposition of a 65% white success rate and a 33% Latinx success rate represents a "critical disturbance" (Engeström 2008), or what John Dewey (in Boydston 1989) called an "indeterminate situation" that calls for inquiry to learn what is going on. To help Burke find out what might be happening in his course, we provided a tool to "code" the names in his grade book by race and ethnicity and use a series of distinct symbols (e.g., a green circle, a red cross) to indicate each student's success, failure, attendance, completion of assignments, etc. Burke discovered that Latinx students had almost perfect attendance, but they were not submitting the homework, which, in turn, may have affected their performance on exams and quizzes. Rather than asking the Latinx students why they were not doing the homework, Burke decided to get the homework started during class, which helped students feel that they could finish it on their own. He also decided to get to know the Latinx students in his class and spend more time speaking with them. The semester after making these and other changes, Burke's data showed an 85.7% success rate for Latinx students, which he attributed to his new practices and more conscious attention to Latinx students.

Advancing from first-generation equity practitioner toward becoming a race-conscious and equity-minded practitioner is not simply a matter of learning new techniques. It requires reflecting on values and beliefs. As Gray shared with us, "Of the many valuable lessons I have learned while working with CUE, no lesson has been as important as realizing that my beliefs, values, and lived experiences serve as the foundation for my words and actions as a teacher." This realization led him to put in writing his commitment to racial equity as the introduction to the tool he created for faculty, *Equity by Design: A Worked Example for Embedding Equity-Minded Practice into the First Three Weeks of Class (Gray, UD)*. See the sidebar for an excerpt of this tool.

A Worked Example for Embedding Equity-Minded Practice into the First Three Weeks of Class

Statement from James Gray, Community College of Aurora Mathematics Faculty and Center for Urban Education Affiliate

My practices are built on the following underlying values and beliefs:

It is my job to be race-conscious. Remaining neutral to, or unaware of, the racialized experiences students have within courses, colleges, other systems of education, and society allows education to reinforce oppression rather than dismantle it.

Education is a human endeavor. My career as a teacher is driven by a passion for the people, not a passion for the subject. Using the words of Rochelle Gutiérrez,[2] it is my job to rehumanize education.

Labeling students as "at-risk," "unprepared," and "coming from a culture that doesn't value education" is inaccurate and dehumanizing. It is my job to disrupt the notion that students deserve the labels others have placed upon them. My belief in my students is unshakable. They have the brilliance, the desire, and the means to be successful.

Educators must learn to be critically race-conscious. First-generation equity practitioners need to learn how to be conscious of their own racial identity and their students' racial identities. Admittedly, it is impossible to know if students are aware of their own racial identity, and if they

---

[2] Rochelle Gutiérrez is a professor at the University of Illinois at Urbana-Champaign. She is the author of "The Sociopolitical Turn in Mathematics Education," *Journal for Research in Mathematics Education* 44 (1): 37–68.

are, how they define it. Nevertheless, practitioners are not color-blind, and they notice who appears to be white, black, Asian, and Latinx. We acknowledge that it is possible that students who are identified as Latinx could be Native American; that students identified as black could be Dominicans, Puerto Ricans, or Cubans; or that students identified as Asian Americans might be Vietnamese or Hmong. Nevertheless, color and ethnicity are present in classrooms, and they shape faculty perceptions (and stereotyping) of students and students' perceptions of faculty and of their peers. Of course, "race" is a socially constructed category; however, as Eduardo Bonilla-Silva points out, it has a "social reality," meaning that "it produces real effects on the actors racialized as 'black' or 'white'" (2006, p. 9).

Research has demonstrated that faculty members' social identities mediate how they experience the classroom and their curricular approaches and pedagogical practices, their interaction with students, and their relationships with colleagues (Chesler and Young 2007). Faculty members' social identities also shape how they perceive student-to-student interactions in the classroom. For example, a black woman faculty member may be more aware of racial and gender dynamics in her classroom than a white male faculty member because she recognizes these instances from her own lived experience (Chesler and Young 2007). Given the multiple ways in which faculty members' social identities shape their own and students' experiences of the classroom, it is important that faculty members reflect on their personal and social identities (Malcom-Piqueux and Bensimon 2017). For an exercise to help first-generation equity practitioners reflect on their racial identity, we recommend the "Social Identity Wheel," an exercise created by the American Association of University Women (n.d.).

To assist you in your journey toward becoming race-conscious and equity-minded, we provide a list of basic practices that will allow you and your colleagues to help racially minoritized students achieve their higher education aspirations:

- Notice the number of students who are white and the number of students who are of color.
- Monitor participation patterns of students by race and ethnicity. Do white males dominate discussions? Are black and Latinx students reluctant to speak out?
- Assess whether you tend to ask complex questions of white students and simple factual questions of nonwhite students.
- Assess if you make assumptions about students' performance and engagement based on race and ethnicity.
- Avoid pedagogical practices that result in the exclusion of minoritized students. For example, when students are asked to form their own groups for an activity, take precautions against students of color being left out or appearing to be "outside" of the group.
- Monitor students' attendance, completion of homework, and performance in quizzes and tests by race and ethnicity to identify patterns that can provide insights into racialized patterns.

Create Syllabi and Materials Reflective of Minoritized Groups

Race-conscious first-generation equity practitioners create syllabi and instructional materials that reflect the culture, history, and contributions of racially minoritized groups. As artifacts of practice, syllabi can reinforce and reproduce the norms and rules that generally align with the experience of white students, or syllabi can counter those norms and rules. For racially or ethnically minoritized students who have experienced exclusion, marginalization, discrimination, and oppression in educational settings and elsewhere, the syllabus is a tool that faculty can use intentionally to demystify the implicit norms and ambiguous processes that need to be learned to navigate college successfully. The content and tone of a syllabus can affirm racially minoritized students that they belong in higher education, confirm their instructors' beliefs that they are expected to succeed, and validate their pursuit of a college degree.

Below is a list of teaching practices that can support the development of race-conscious practitioners among first-generation equity instructors.

Ensure that minoritized students see themselves in syllabi, assignments, and other instructional materials (texts, videos, special projects, etc.). Instructors can accomplish this by selecting readings and types of assignments, or by not evading materials or discussions of the United States' history of racism, genocide, and colonization or contemporary issues such as anti-immigration policies, racial profiling, and miscarriages of justice.

Make race visible in syllabi by including texts, videos, and other teaching artifacts authored by racially minoritized scholars, authors, and cultural critics. For example: including bell hooks's *Teaching to Transgress: Education as a Practice of Freedom* in education courses; the novels and poetry of Native American author Louise Erdrich in English courses; Ava DuVernay's documentaries *13th* and *When They See Us* in sociology and law courses; Tomas Rivera's *And the Earth Did Not Devour Him* in literature courses; Cherrie Moraga and Gloria Anzaldúa's *This Bridge Called My Back* in philosophy courses; Laura Rendón's *From the Barrio to the Academy: Revelations of a Mexican American "Scholarship Girl"* in education courses and student success courses; Viet Than Nguyen's novel *The Sympathizer* in history and English courses.

The purpose of this list is not to single out these works as essential. They are examples to provide guidance, and instructors should assume the responsibility of making judgments about what is relevant to include.

Create a learning plan to become familiar with minoritized writers, poets, sociologists, political scientists, philosophers, scientists, mathematicians, artists, and musicians. As first-generation equity practitioners, instructors have to invest time in learning what they have not been taught. Recommendations to revise courses and curricula to be more racially inclusive are often met with comments such as "This is not my area of expertise," "This is not what I know," or "I don't have room for anything else." One of the advantages of technology is that it is easy to do searches to identify black sociologists, Native American and Latinx authors, or Asian American historians. There are many helpful websites with materials, and disciplinary associations often address issues of diversity in the curriculum. It takes the will to get out of one's comfort zone and explore new knowledge and entertain new perspectives.

Apply the questions below to assess ways in which your syllabi communicate the value of students' racial/ethnic backgrounds as sources of learning and language:[3]

- Does your syllabus acknowledge that student learning benefits from deep and rich engagement of students' racial or ethnic backgrounds and experiences?
- Does it include a statement that recognizes the value of the racial or ethnic backgrounds and experiences that all students bring into the learning environment?
- Does it include readings, activities, and assignments that are culturally relevant and inclusive (e.g., those that incorporate issues of race or ethnicity, gender, language, sexuality, and disability to show a diversity of perspectives and lived experiences)?
- Does it include multiple assignments or discussion topics that allow students to share and draw on their experiential knowledge and/or the knowledge of their communities?
- Does it include multiple topics and assignments on the real-world problems and issues facing the communities or cultural groups from which students come?

---

[3] These questions were drawn from the Center for Urban Education's Syllabus Review Protocol available at http://cue.usc.edu.

Final Thoughts

At the height of the US civil rights movement, Dr. Martin Luther King Jr. (1963) said, "Rarely do we find men who willingly engage in hard, solid thinking. There is an almost universal quest for easy answers and half-baked solutions. Nothing pains some people more than having to think." Our insistence on the urgent need to develop equity-minded capacity among practitioners is because, like Dr. King, we find it is rare for institutional stakeholders to willingly engage in hard thinking about their practices and how they contribute to racist outcomes. To paraphrase Dr. King, we are witnessing in higher education "an almost universal quest for structural and technical solutions" that fail to confront the real problem underlying racial inequality: whiteness. We have provided a strategy that is inspired by the power of learning as a means of practitioner self-change. Our conception of first-generation equity practitioners represents a quest for a solution to racial inequity that empowers professionals to remake their practices.

References

AAC&U (Association of American Colleges and Universities). 2007. "The essential learning outcomes." https://www.aacu.org/sites/default/files/files/LEAP/EssentialOutcomes_Chart.pdf (accessed September 2019).

AAC&U (Association of American Colleges and Universities) (2015a). *Committing to Equity and Inclusive Excellence: Campus Guide for Self-Study and Planning*. Washington, DC: Association of American Colleges and Universities https://www.aacu.org/sites/default/files/CommittingtoEquityInclusiveExcellence.pdf.

AAC&U (Association of American Colleges and Universities) (2015b). *Step Up and Lead for Equity: What Higher Education Can Do to Reverse Our Deepening Divides*. Washington, DC: Association of American Colleges and Universities.

AAC&U (Association of American Colleges and Universities) (2015c). *The LEAP Challenge: Education for a World of Unscripted Problems*. Washington, DC: Association of American Colleges and Universities https://www.aacu.org/sites/default/files/files/LEAP/LEAPChallengeBrochure.pdf.

AAC&U (Association of American Colleges and Universities) (2018). *A Vision for Equity*. Washington, DC: AAC&U.

AAC&U (Association of American Colleges and Universities). 2019. "2019 diversity, equity, and student success." https://www.aacu.org/conferences/dess/2019 (accessed July 25, 2019).

AAC&U (Association of American Colleges and Universities). n.d. "Making Excellence Inclusive." https://www.aacu.org/making-excellence-inclusive (accessed July 25, 2019).

American Association of University Women. n.d. "Diversity and inclusion tool kit." https://aauw-pa.aauw.net/files/2012/02/DI-Toolkit-nsa.pdf (accessed July 25, 2019).

Badger, Emily. 2015. "Black poverty differs from white poverty." *Washington Post.* (August 12). https://www.washingtonpost.com/news/wonk/wp/2015/08/12/black-poverty-differs-from-white-poverty (accessed July 25, 2019).

Bauer-Wolf, Jeremy. 2019. "#DoesUIowaLoveMe." *Inside Higher Ed.* (Feburary 27). https://www.insidehighered.com/news/2019/02/27/u-iowa-students-launch-digital-campaign-around-minority-issues-campus (accessed July 25, 2019).

Bauman, G.L. (2005). Promoting organizational learning in higher education to achieve equity in educational outcomes. *New Directions for Higher Education* 2005 (131): 23–35.

Bensimon, E.M. (2007). The underestimated significance of practitioner knowledge in the scholarship of student success. *Review of Higher Education* 30 (4): 441–469.

Bensimon, E.M. (2012). The equity scorecard: theory of change. In: *Confronting Equity Issues on Campus: Implementing the Equity Scorecard in Theory and Practice* (eds. E. Mara and L. Malcom), 17–44.

Bensimon, Estela Mara. 2015. Unpublished memo to a Provost.

Bensimon, E.M. (2016). *The Misbegotten URM as a Data Point.* Los Angeles, CA: Center for Urban Education, Rossier School of Education, University of Southern California.

Bensimon, E.M. (2018). Reclaiming racial justice in equity. *Change: The Magazine of Higher Learning* 50 (3–4): 95–98.

Bensimon, E.M., Dowd, A.C., and Witham, K. (2016). Five principles for enacting equity by design. *Diversity & Democracy* 19 (1) https://www.aacu.org/diversitydemocracy/2016/winter/bensimon.

Bensimon, E.M., Dowd, A.C., Stanton-Salazar, R.D., and Davila, B. (2019). The role of institutional agents in providing institutional support to Latino students in STEM. *Review of Higher Education* 42 (4): 1689–1721.

Bensimon, E.M. and Harris, F. III. (2012). The mediational mean of enacting equity-mindedness among community college practitioners. In: *Confronting Equity Issues on Campus: Implementing the Equity Scorecard in Theory and Practice* (eds. E.M. Bensimon and L.E. Malcom), 216–246. Sterling, VA: Stylus Publishing.

Bensimon, E.M. and Malcom, L. (2012). *Confronting Equity Issues on Campus: Implementing the Equity Scorecard in Theory and Practice.* Sterling, VA: Stylus.

Bensimon, E.M., Polkinghorne, D.E., Bauman, G.L., and Vallejo, E. (2004). Doing research that makes a difference. *Journal of Higher Education 75* (1): 104–126.

Berrett, D. (2015). Stunned by a video, University of Oklahoma Struggles to talk about race. *Chronicle of Higher Education* https://www.chronicle.com/article/Stunned-by-a-Video-U-of/228611.

Bonilla-Silva, E. (2006). *Racism without Racists: Color-Blind Racism and the Persistence of Racial Inequality in the United States*, 2e. Lanham: Rowman & Littlefield Publishers.

Boydston, J. (ed.) (1989). *The Later Works of John Dewey, 1925–1953*, vol. 8. Carbondale: Southern Illinois University Press.

Bustillos, L.T., Rueda, R., and Bensimon, E.M. (2011). Faculty views of under-represented students in community college settings: cultural models and cultural practices. In: *Vygotsky in 21st Century Society: Advances in Cultural Historical Theory and Praxis with Non-Dominant Communities* (eds. P. Portes and S. Salas), 199–213. New York: Peter Lang.

Cahalan, M., Perna, L.W., Yamashita, M. et al. (2018). *Indicators of Higher Education Equity in the United States: 2018 Historical Trend Report*. Washington, DC: Pell Institute for the Study of Opportunity in Higher Education, Council for Opportunity in Education, and Alliance for Higher Education and Democracy of the University of Pennsylvania.

Carter, P.L., Skiba, R., Arredondo, M.I., and Pollock, M. (2017). You can't fix what you don't look at: acknowledging race in addressing racial discipline disparities. *Urban Education* 52 (2): 207–235.

Center for Urban Education (2019). *Student Equity Planning Institute*. Los Angeles: Center for Urban Education at the University of Southern California, Rossier School of Education.

Chesler, M. and Young, A.A. Jr. (2007). Faculty members' social identities and classroom authority. *New Directions for Teaching and Learning* 111: 11–19.

Cohen, D.K., Raudenbush, S.W., and Ball, D.L. (2003). Resources, instruction, and research. *Educational Evaluation and Policy Analysis 25* (2): 119–142.

Dey, E. (2009). Another inconvenient truth: capturing campus climate and its consequences. *Diversity & Democracy* 12 (1): 10–11.

DiAngelo, R. (2011). White fragility. *International Journal of Critical Pedagogy* 3 (3): 54–70.

Dowd, Alicia C. and Bensimon, E. M. (2012). "What's Race Got to Do with It?" *American Educational Research Association (AERA)*. https://www.aera.net/Events-Meetings/Annual-Meeting/Previous-Annual-Meetings/2013-Annual-Meeting/Responses-to-the-2013-Annual-Meeting-Theme/Whats-Race-Got-to-Do-with-It/articleType/ArticleView/articleId/1175/Whats-Race-Got-to-Do-with-It- (accessed July 25, 2019).

Dowd, A.C. and Bensimon, E.M. (2015). *Engaging the "Race Question": Accountability and Equity in U.S. Higher Education*, Multicultural Education Series. New York: Teachers College Press.

Dowd, A.C., Witham, K., Hanson, D. et al. (2018). *Bringing Accountability to Life: How Savvy Data Users Find the "Actionable N" to Improve Equity and Sustainability in Higher Education*. Washington, DC: American Council on Education, The Pennsylvania State University Center for the Study of Higher Education, and the University of Southern California Center for Urban Education.

Du Bois, W.E.B. (1903) 1994. *The Souls of Black Folk*. New York: Dover Publications.

Ekowo, M. and Palmer, I. (2016). *The Promise and Peril of Predictive Analytics in Higher Education: A Landscape Analysis*. Washington, DC: The New America Foundation.

Engeström, Y. (2001). Expansive learning at work: toward an activity theoretical reconceptualization. *Journal of Education and Work 14* (1): 133–156.

Engeström, Y. (2008). *From Teams to Knots: Activity-Theoretical Studies of Collaboration and Learning at Work*. Cambridge, UK: Cambridge University Press.

Espinosa, L.L., Turk, J.M., Taylor, M., and Chessman, H.M. (2019). *Race and Ethnicity in Higher Education: A Status Report*. Washington, DC: American Council on Education.

Essed, P. (1991). *Understanding Everyday Racism: An Interdisciplinary Approach*. London: Sage.

Felix, E.R., Bensimon, E.M., Hanson, D. et al. (2015). Developing Agency for Equity-Minded Change. In: *Understanding Equity in Community College Practice* (ed. E.L. Castro). San Francisco: Wiley Periodicals.

Finley, A. and McNair, T.B. (2013). *Assessing Underserved Students' Engagement in High-Impact Practices*. Washington, DC: Association of American Colleges and Universities.

Frankenberg, R. (1993). *White Women, Race Matter: The Social Construction of Whiteness*. Minneapolis: University of Minnesota Press.

Harper, S.R. (2010). An anti-deficit achievement framework for research on students of color in STEM. In: *Students of Color in STEM: Engineering a New Research Agenda, New Directions for Institutional Research* (eds. S.R. Harper and C.B. Newman). San Francisco: Jossey-Bass.

Harper, S.R. (2012). Race without racism: how higher education researchers minimize racist institutional norms. *Review of Higher Education 36* (1): 9–29.

Hart Research Associates (2015). *Bringing Equity and Quality Learning Together: Institutional Priorities for Tracking and Advancing Underserved Students' Success*. Washington, DC: Association of American Colleges and Universities.

Heutsche, A.M. and Hicks, K. (2018). Embedding equity through the practice of real talk. In: *A Vision for Equity: Results from AAC&U's Project: Committing to Equity and Inclusive Excellence: Campus-Based Strategies for Student Success*. Washington, DC: Association of American Colleges.

Johnson, Lyndon. 1965. "To Fulfill These Rights." Commencement address, Howard University. June 4. Transcript published in Blackpast. May 27, 2010. https://www.blackpast.org/african-american-history/1965-president-lyndon-b-johnson-fulfill-these-rights-3.

Kemmis, S. and McTaggart, R. (2000). Participatory action research. In: *Handbook of Qualitative Research*, 2e (eds. N. Denzin and Y. Lincoln). Thousand Oaks, CA: Sage Publications.

Kuh, G.D. (2008). *High-Impact Educational Practices: What They Are, Who Has Access to Them, and Why They Matter*. Washington, DC: Association of American Colleges and Universities.

Kuh, G.D. and O'Donnell, K. (2013). *Ensuring Quality & Taking High-Impact Practices to Scale*. Washington, DC: Association of American Colleges and Universities.

Ladson-Billings, G. (2006). From the achievement gap to the education debt: understanding achievement in U.S. schools. *Educational Researcher* 35 (7): 3–12.

Malcom-Piqueux, L.E. and Bensimon, E.M. (2017). Taking equity-minded action to close equity gaps. *Peer Review* 19 (2): 5–8.

Mangan, Katherine. 2019. "Another Blackface Incident Sends U. of Oklahoma Students Reeling." *Chronicle of Higher Education*. https://www.chronicle.com/article/Another-Blackface-Incident/245538 (accessed July 25, 2019).

Martin Luther King Jr. (1963). *Strength to Love*. New York: Harper & Row.

McIntosh, P. (1988). White privilege and male privilege: a personal account of coming to see correspondence through work in Women's studies. In: *Race, Class, and Gender: An Anthology*, 9e (eds. M.L. Anderson and P.H. Collins). Boston: Cengage Learning.

McIntosh, P. (2019). White privilege: Unpacking the invisible knapsack. In: *Race, Class, and Gender: An Anthology* (eds. M.L. Anderson and P.H. Collins). Belmont, CA: Wadsworth https://www.racialequitytools.org/resourcefiles/mcintosh.pdf.

McIntyre, A. (1997). *Making Meaning of Whiteness: Exploring Racial Identity with White Teachers*. State University of New York Press.

McPherson, L.K. (2015). Righting historical injustice in higher education. In: *The Aims of Higher Education: Problems of Morality and Justice* (eds. H. Brighouse and M. McPherson). Chicago: University of Chicago Press.

Peña, E.V. (2012). Inquiry methods for critical consciousness and self-change in faculty. *The Review of Higher Education 36* (1).

Perakyla, A. (2005). Analyzing talk and text. In: *The Sage Handbook of Qualitative Research*, 3e (eds. N. Denzin and Y. Lincoln). Thousand Oaks, CA: Sage Publications.

Polkinghorne, D.E. (2004). *Practice and the Human Sciences: The Case for a Judgment-Based Practice of Care*. Albany: State University of New York Press.

Pollock, M. (2009). *Colormute: Race Talk Dilemmas in an American School*. Princeton, NJ: Princeton University Press.

Wilder, C. (2013). *Ebony and Ivy: Race, Slavery, and the Troubled History of America's Universities*. New York: Bloomsbury Press.

Witham, K. and Bensimon, E.M. (2012). Creating a culture of inquiry around equity and student success. In: *Creating Campus Cultures: Fostering Success among Racially Diverse Student Populations* (eds. S.D. Museus and U.M. Jayakumar). New York: Routledge.

Witham, K., Malcom-Piqueux, L.E., Dowd, A.C., and Bensimon, E.M. (2015). *America's Unmet Promise: The Imperative for Equity in Higher Education*. Washington, DC: Association of American Colleges and Universities.

Index